WITH

GARDEN DESIGN BY FIONA BROCKHOFF

NATURE

PHOTOGRAPHY BY EARL CARTER

Hardie Grant

BOOKS

I would like to acknowledge the country and traditional owners of the land we live, work, and learn on, the Wurundjeri and Bunurong people, as well as the people of the wider Kulin Nations.

We pay our respects to elders, past, present, and emerging.

Aboriginal peoples have lived on this land for over 60,000 years and to this day remain one of the longest and oldest living cultures in the world. We acknowledge that this land was never ceded, and recognise the ongoing connection of Indigenous people, to this land and its waters, and celebrate their enduring practices, presence, and knowledge.

This always was, always will be Aboriginal land.

In exploring indigenous lands, practices, and knowledge systems, we hope to educate ourselves and others better, and recognise we are limited as we speak only from own positions, perspectives, experiences and biases. We do not intend to speak over or replace the voices of indigenous peoples and traditional custodians in this sharing of knowledge and are grateful for the continuation of knowledge sharing that has been left to us by those who have passed into their Ancestral Dreaming.

IN MEMORY OF MY MUM, NYON BROCKHOFF,
WHO SOWED THE CREATIVE SEEDS IN MY LIFE.

TO DAVID SWANN, MY PARTNER IN LOVE AND WORK,
WHOSE SUPERB EYE AND HARD WORK ARE BEHIND
MANY OF MY GARDENS.

MY JOURNEY WITH PLANTS

GARDEN DESIGN

THE
GARDENS

INTRODUCTION

With Nature is a book for garden makers and land carers far and wide. It contains help and inspiration for anyone creating a garden anywhere. It coalesces an approach to garden design that can be applied to or adopted wherever you may be living – a courtyard garden can give as much enjoyment and fulfilment as acreage and, indeed, when space is limited, it could be said that it's even more important to actively design your garden.

As a garden designer, I have been commissioned to work on many sites across south-eastern Australia. However, for the last twenty-five years I have specialised in coastal gardens, stemming from living in Sorrento, on Victoria's Mornington Peninsula. I became recognised for much of this coastal work and for the creation of our own garden there, Karkalla.

From an early age I wondered about how much time my dad put into maintaining a green lawn. Watering, mowing, fertilising and coring compacted areas were all regular activities. Yes, we children loved rolling and running around on that lawn, but, even then, I puzzled over just how much of a battle it seemed to be, to force this patch of grass into service. Later I would wonder at what expense to the health of our planet, too.

In my teens and throughout my training in horticulture, my eyes were opened to the natural world. Arguably my love of gardening came later. Through hiking and bushwalking I essentially fell in love with the shape, colour, habits and distribution of Australian native plants in the wild – the spaces they lived in, the rocks and lichens, the effect of wind, altitude and grazing animals: in short, the environment. Reading about and then visiting famous gardens, gazing at beautiful, simple and robust Mediterranean terraced spaces – just so *right* for the place – was a revelation.

From that moment on I have believed that beautiful, functional gardens are not resource hungry. It is a matter of careful site observation, sensible design and utilising local materials. And it applies to every garden situation, regardless of its size or location.

The final critical element is choosing plants that have a good ecological fit with your garden space. Curate plant species that will grow easily, in a style you enjoy, rather than attempting to change your site to grow whatever you want, regardless of requirements. Designing gardens *with* nature, to suit the environment and create a strong sense of place, is about being respectful and sensible. Imagination is the only limiting factor.

With Nature has three sections. The first explores my early influences and journey as an observant lover of nature, gardener, then garden designer. My success as a garden designer is in large part due to those other two strong threads in my life. This section also charts the birth and development of Karkalla.

In the second part of the book I explain the most important principles and elements in my approach to garden design, including how to assess a site's potential, choose materials and the importance of space, texture and arrangement in a design.

The final section of the book includes my signature plant list and profiles thirteen gardens: large and small coastal sites, country, as well as inner city and urban garden designs. The idea of this book has had a long genesis because I wanted to wait for some of the gardens to reach a certain maturity to be included here. They are now of age: the oldest garden shown here is fifteen years old, the youngest only three.

MY JOURNEY
WITH PLANTS

ABOVE Perched on a rock near an alpine bog below the summit of
Mount Feathertop. For me, immersion in nature is inspiring and the hike
to get there fulfilling (photographs pages 10 and 12 Tamsin O'Neill).

HOW I CAME TO LOVE PLANTS

My first memory is of a plant. Outside my cot window was a grouping of aloes. I remember gazing through the bars of my cot at these spiky plants and their colourful flowers that grew right up to my window.

My parents were both keen gardeners. My father, Alan, was a lawn man; the greener the better, and he designed a sophisticated irrigation system that ensured this. Summer evenings were spent tending to this lawn, by the seaside in Portsea, and making sure cars in the driveway were parked on the random stepping stones of slate rather than on his magnificent lawn. My mother, Nyon, on the other hand was a creative soul and involved herself in designing and tending a garden that complemented our 1959 vanilla brick Modernist home in inner Melbourne. Mum had wanted to study architecture after completing school; however, her father, with strict views on what vocations were appropriate for young women of the 1940s, believed that becoming an architect was definitely not suitable for his daughter. Mum later satisfied, to a degree, her creative desires through gardening, knitting, sewing and the design and interior furnishing of our home.

Our Melbourne garden was a clever combination of Mum's childhood favourites with the more architectural plants of the day. This is where my love affair with flax, *Tetrapanax papyrifer*, strelitzia, agave, aloe, aeonium and other succulents began. It was also in this garden that I learnt about the delicious scents of spring flowering jasmine, winter honeysuckle, mock orange, magnolia and daphne – scents that today trigger immediate memories of Mum. The garden also displayed a variety of textures in its hard landscape. Crazy paving, stacked slate walls and pebbles embedded in concrete all played roles in creating something that pushed the conventional garden boundaries of the 1940s and 50s.

I loved our light-filled modern home where textures were celebrated and innovative design was integrated into everything. This approach made our smallish house feel large, since everything was considered; everything had a place or a home. As I got older my friends laughed and called it 'the *Brady Bunch* house' but I secretly loved its open-plan living and bright spaces that blended so well with the garden. Colour was important to Mum, and she celebrated this in the home and garden spaces, and in so doing created strong connections between both. All these considerations and design responses, I now realise, clearly influenced how I design gardens and the integration of the houses that partner them: thoughtfully designed, cohesive, minimalistic spaces that are decorated by particular plant communities.

Television in our house was strictly regulated as Mum believed it killed children's creativity. This belief, coupled with primary schooling at Preshil (a small, independent coeducational school in Kew, where creativity and independence are encouraged regardless of age), meant that my siblings and I were often left to our own devices to create: paint, draw, garden, build cubby houses … Much of my childhood was spent fiddling in the garden, where I created miniature moss gardens, homes for pet frogs under the trampoline and wove mats from strappy garden plants like flax and winter iris. I loved tree climbing, my favourite being a large ghost maple that dominated our rear garden, and once up in its lofty branches I became lost in another world. Clambering onto the flat roof of our house provided another vantage point and from this height I could see every corner of the garden and its plants. One of my favourite activities was to help our housekeeper Andy tend to her numerous pots of fuchsias that she kept on her east-facing balcony. She loved the frilly, garishly coloured cultivars, and although not to my liking, involvement in their care alongside Andy made me happy. Also under my watchful eye was a collection of African violets, planted in a set of beautifully painted Portuguese pots inherited from Gran, which lived on the kitchen windowsill with just the right amount of sunlight to thrive.

MY JOURNEY WITH PLANTS

ABOVE White-trunked *Betula utilis* var. *jacquemontii* in the central courtyard are repeated in the rear garden to create continuity. On this wet site it was easy to create a lush green display of tumbling ground covers, succulents, tussocks and shrubs, many originating from Asia.

ABOVE Textured surfaces, organic shapes and natural forms are trademarks of the landscape design at Karkalla; the walls of local limestone are a spine to the house. They link external and internal spaces and provide vital protection from ocean winds.

During this early time elderly great-aunt Ethel Barnes was also a welcome presence and inspiration in our lives. Ethel was a sculptor and an eccentric, counting the famous sculptor Clifford Last as a close friend and creative influence, and she enjoyed filling her home and garden with pieces she had made or collected on her travels. Ethel had a fierce determination about her despite her petite frame, and she showed us that women were capable of almost anything – and at any age. She moved to America aged 101 to be closer to her elderly daughter. She left an enormous void in our lives when she died.

At thirteen I discovered the Australian bush. My father's health was failing, and I was sent to board at Geelong Grammar School's campus, Timbertop. The bush campus is between Mansfield and the base of Mount Buller in the Victorian Alps, and it was a turning point for me. For an entire school year students live together in small self-contained cabins of fourteen to sixteen people. Activities are centred around the local environment, outdoor education and being part of a small community. Students hike, run, camp, ski, canoe, learn bush skills and work on local farms while undertaking academic studies. It was a tough year both physically and mentally for me but the sense of achievement by the end was enormous. Creating a geological collection from all the local rock types, collating an insect display and making a table from a site-grown pine tree was a dream come true for me. I learnt about Indigenous and colonial history, studied different communities of flora and fauna and recorded weather observations, including monitoring temperatures and cloud identification. These were activities that took my schoolwork in a whole new direction; I was not complaining.

Like many experiences, I didn't realise at the time the influence this year would have on the rest of my life; it was the first time I had been fully immersed in the Australian bush for a period longer than a weekend camping trip or a visit to a friend's holiday shack in the country. This was the real deal. I discovered I had an eye for detail and had begun to observe the minutiae and intricacies of this natural world and notice things about its rhythms that were unobtainable in the city.

My love of hiking was born during that year of camping and countless hikes. I had plenty of opportunities to observe naturally occurring plant communities, especially in alpine and montane areas, and the conditions in which they thrived. I found this firsthand experience of plants enthralling, an extension of my early garden enthusiasms at home. This new-found interest applied to eucalypts and the large range of species we came across hiking, from the gnarled snow gums (*Eucalyptus pauciflora*) above the snow line, to the valleys of towering mountain ash (*E. regnans*) at lower elevations. Expansive drifts of snow daisies (*Celmisia*), plains of alpine grasses, outcrops of rocks covered in tapestries of lichen and the glory of spring wattle all left a lasting impression on me. I saw beauty everywhere there, and it was that year that helped open my eyes to the natural way of things. When I reflect back, the experience of that pristine environment, combined with a love of creating, led with time to my career in landscape design. Not surprisingly, art, ceramics, biology and geography remained my favourite subjects during my later years at school at the Corio campus near Geelong.

My path toward becoming a landscape designer was never linear. After a false start in the Commerce/Arts Faculties at Melbourne University I enrolled in a Degree of Applied Science (Horticulture) at Burnley campus. There I was enthusiastic from the start, learning everything I could about plants, then plants in design at a later stage. I loved all the offered subjects that related to plants; Plant Identification was one of my favourites and every week we studied twenty new plants. I was excited to be learning about species' origins, what conditions they like to grow in and their attributes. I was also learning how plants functioned in Plant Physiology, how to propagate them in Nursery Propagation and Management, how to maintain them in a horticultural setting, and how they might be included in a garden design context. One of our early assignments involved creating a planting scheme for a small plot, the sole brief to create year-round interest. My scheme was simple and involved silver birches and *Acanthus mollis* as the stars. I recall feeling quite pleased with the design – although I have no memory of feedback or assessment. But the die was cast. The subject of design engaged me more than anything else: I had found a career path that combined my love of design, plants and the natural world.

During the four-year course we studied gardens from all over the world and visited many in and around Melbourne. I could not fail to notice that much of what we visited was in large part copied in style from abroad. Where were the uniquely Australian gardens, I wondered, celebrating our own diverse flora? There were copies of Sissinghurst's famous White Garden, miniature Japanese gardens, herbaceous borders in the English style and formal Italianate arrangements. Australia, it seemed, was deferring to what was going on in the rest of the world in terms of garden trends and ideas. This was also the case in other fields: Australia had not yet found the confidence to develop its own style and expression in design.

But there were some Australian gardens and gardeners that made an impression on me during my studies. At one garden in the Dandenong Ranges, today known as Karwarra Australian Plant Garden, native flora was and still is celebrated with style and a casual ease. I was also influenced by the work of Edna Walling. English-born Walling's gardens generally relied on strong architectural components that celebrated local slate and other stones, over which she established a soft mantle of planting. She allowed plants to make their own pictures and relied on the built structure to visually hold them together.

ABOVE Australian native correas, lomandras and kangaroo grass play a role in a modern Japanese aesthetic. The upright spikes of *Phormium tenax* 'Anna Red' sit in front of warm-toned *Agonis flexuosa* 'Burgundy' and a deciduous *Cercis canadensis* 'Forest Pansy'. An existing *Jacaranda mimosifolia* provides an important canopy.

19

ABOVE Copses of *Tetrapanax papyrifer* create an eye-catching canopy and provide important shade with its giant leaves. Its reptilian trunks provide texture at eye level.

Towards the end of her career Walling began using Australian plant species, especially at Bickleigh Vale in Mooroolbark, her vision for an English-style village. For my final-year dissertation at Burnley I developed a restoration management plan for a Walling garden.

Halfway through my degree, in 1985, I took a gap year to work and later travel in the UK and parts of Europe and visit dozens of gardens. Initially I studied with John Brookes, a well-known British landscape designer who ran design courses from his home and studio, Clock House, near Chichester, West Sussex. Here I boarded with a local family and attended John's studio each day with ten other students from around the world, in a stimulating and intensive learning environment. He critiqued our designs for invented briefs (conveniently there was never a budget). John would describe a site and provide us with a survey and a thorough brief to work with; once complete, the design was presented to the group for feedback. Along with visiting local landscapes both private and municipal, John taught us design techniques that I use to this day. It was at Clock House that I first saw 'gravel gardening' being used, a technique initially championed by Beth Chatto in a horticultural situation and since adopted by many. The approach made perfect sense to me, and I could see how we might use gravel as mulch and a practical surface material in our landscape designs and our dry climates in Australia. What if we used fine seas of gravel as an open-space material, rather than traditional lawns that were resource hungry? It was an idea that I would first experiment with in Albury five years later.

The best part of my year abroad was that it also gave me an opportunity to visit many of the UK's famous gardens such as Sissinghurst, Great Dixter and several of the celebrated landscapes of Capability Brown. These were gardens I had read about extensively but now had the chance to wander through and experience. Seeing these beautiful English gardens in situ drove home the folly of replicating a garden style and slavishly using plant species in Australia that were not suited to either our lifestyle or our climate.

When I visited Mediterranean countries, including Greece, Turkey and Italy, it was obvious to me that many of the plant species endemic to these regions shared climatic conditions and geology similar to many parts of Australia. The warmer temperatures made for a more relaxed approach to life and the design of domestic gardens and houses reflected this. People's use of plants in these dry climates and their approach to landscape design and architecture had great relevance to Australian conditions and circumstances.

I returned home enthusiastic about everything I'd seen and keen to design landscapes that were suited to our more informal, outdoor-orientated lifestyle and in keeping with Melbourne's temperate climes. Without question, the time spent studying with

RIGHT Clinging *Parthenocissus tricuspidata* greens and softens an entrance, with *Nandina domestica* and *Dietes iridioides* 'White Tiger', repeated inside. The slate paving and decorative wrought iron gate draw visitors through to the treed garden within.

John Brookes, as well as seeing for myself a huge variety of landscapes – both man-made and natural – had made an enormous impact on me.

Two years later I graduated from Burnley and found work with an inner-city retail nursery. Town and Country Gardens offered a landscape design service, and it was there I began to practise and hone my design skills. Serving customers in the nursery, and through their common questions, I got to know what many people wanted in terms of plants and landscape ideas. I lived nearby in Prahran, in a Victorian weatherboard terrace house, among a large Greek community. These neighbours really knew the meaning of the word 'community'. Front and rear gardens were given over to food production. Rows of onions grew alongside staked carnations in front of small and large Victorian villas, laden olive trees leant over footpaths and lemons grew abundantly and were gifted generously. Plants and produce were

ABOVE Karkalla's kitchen garden is packed with vegetables, herbs, flowers and plants to attract beneficial insects. Salad-ready greens grow easily, and self-seeding is encouraged in both the concrete beds and in the fine seas of gravel beneath

a language we all had in common. I had loved travelling in Greece – the climate, the landscape, the lifestyle – and I attempted to capture that, in a modified fashion, in suburban Prahran.

Quickly, the large rectangle of dry lawn at the rear of my house became a productive kitchen garden. A pergola was added to the west, grapevines planted to cover it, lemon trees sourced, and every type of vegetable and herb planted. Olive trees flanked my newly painted, Greek blue front door, and lessons were forthcoming as to how I should brine the fruit.

When I moved from Prahran to Albury in late 1989 to get married so did the source of much of my design work. My then mother-in-law had me consulting for her gardening friends, both out on farms and in town. Those commissions and resulting referrals were most welcome, and I soon found myself busily engaged in landscape designing, sourcing and using indigenous plant species and other species tolerant of the hot dry summers and cold winters.

I loved the way of life I was discovering and the resourceful and practical approach to gardening and planting design I found there. Plants were often shared as cuttings rather than purchased; kitchen gardens and orchards were commonplace and dynamic; materials were locally sourced or repurposed. Plants were selected because they thrived without much intervention in the given circumstances, and I continued in that vein, using local species *Eucalyptus siderox-ylon*, bottlebrush, correa, various tussocks and many members of the Rosaceae family including pear, apple, quince and species roses. Mediterranean plants also featured, especially if the site was frost-free, and I used lavender, rosemary, phlomis and other old-fashioned shrubs that were reliable and Walling favourites. If revegetation of degraded areas in paddocks was required or establishment of windbreaks, I always sought indigenous plant species.

I thought carefully about the design and plant choices I was making. I was a city girl newly arrived in the country, and I did not want to be branded as having outlandish, impractical or expensive design ideas. I wanted my design practice to thrive and to establish myself as a local landscape designer who could deliver practical, economically built, beautiful gardens.

We spent weekends skiing in the Victorian Alps, hiking and camping in the bush or along the Murray River. I loved these excursions off the beaten track where I could observe and interact with nature firsthand, harking back to my immersion at Timbertop, but this time with the eyes of a landscape designer. There was so much to see and learn in nature's arrangements of plant communities. Around this time, I enrolled in a master of permaculture course in nearby Chiltern where Vries Gravenstein, a Dutch-born permaculturist, taught from his small farm. Here I met other enthusiasts interested in 'stepping lightly on the world' through creating logically arranged organic food production systems, strawbale housing, recycling, and sustainable water and sewage systems. I'd already seen a similar resourcefulness at work in the sensible arrangement of elements on many of the farms I was visiting: chook runs adjacent to vegetable gardens and orchards, a clothes line on the way to both and a composting area. Permaculture expanded on these ideas and gave it a name. It was also against chemical use in terms of plant sprays, herbicides and animal drenches and this was a big change to normal practices.

It was at our newly acquired Modernist-inspired Albury house that I excitedly designed my first larger-scale gravel garden. Our site was steep and abutted natural bushland, with granitic soils and rocky outcrops. Again, the lawns were removed, replaced with seas of fine granite gravel from a nearby quarry. In my Prahran garden I'd loved the profusion of self-seeding that occurred on the paths I'd made between the beds. Thyme, lavender, lettuces, olives, parsley, fennel – almost everything loved to germinate in the moist, mineral-rich gravel given the chance. As soon as we had put the gravel in place in Albury, plants indigenous to the region, including those occurring in the bushland behind us, began to make themselves at home.

We constructed a natural-style pond in the rear garden at the base of a large granitic rock face. Water ran down the face of the rock – itself a beautiful sculptural element – and was then recirculated. We planted various indigenous plant species in and around the body of water. Lizards and other reptiles, frogs and an abundance of birdlife all enjoyed this welcome new ecosystem. Even wallabies, especially in summer when it was hot and dry, would occasionally find their way to our waterhole. We were working with nature and all she had to offer.

In creating our own naturalistic garden in Albury, I ended up trying and testing a number of design and growing ideas based on gravel and native plants. There were wins and losses, and I reflected on them all before I arrived at a number of design ideas that still shape my work today. Growing the plants in gravel meant no garden edging was required because open, flat gravel seas transitioned seamlessly into the plantings themselves. The garden bed soil did not require cultivating or mulching since the gravel *was* mulch. Once the plantings began to establish, I began pruning some of the shrubs into domed shapes. This visually anchored the scene – otherwise there was a risk it could look like a revegetation project. Mass planting of single plant species such as grasses and ground covers gave the garden scene a simpler, stronger look. Training and selectively pruning the trees, including the existing eucalypts, into sculptural forms provided further cohesion. Although I was not to see this garden mature past two years, this approach turned out to be easy, and the garden was visually appealing and not difficult to manage.

RIGHT A deep bed of dense planting near the front of the house is filled with deliberate layers of height, visual interest and biodiversity. The retained *Leptospermum laevigatum* shade and shelter the house as well as provide privacy.

ABOVE Carefully considered architecture brings the garden into the home and maximises natural light in this stairwell.

WHY GARDEN?

I believe gardening is almost part of our DNA. Humans have been cultivating plants for various purposes since we headed to the plains from the forests; it is something we do instinctively if given the opportunity and a small amount of space. In today's fast-paced world, gardening remains an opportunity to connect with nature and its natural rhythms. It is a chance to observe, create and produce something that gives pleasure and benefits whether that be for animal habitat, human shelter, recreation, relaxation, to grow food or simply for beauty. There are many worthwhile reasons to garden.

All plants sequestrate carbon dioxide from the atmosphere and store it in the soil carbon pool. This function is mediated by a plant's extraordinary process of photosynthesis, and most life on Earth depends on it. For this reason alone, cultivating a diversity of plants such as ground covers, tussocks, shrubs, trees and aquatic species is of the utmost importance if we're going to save our world for future generations.

Gardening is good for your mental health and emotional wellbeing. The mere task of tending to a single pot plant on a windowsill can be rewarding. Watering, feeding, training and ensuring adequate sunlight for this single living organism can give pleasure and purpose as well as cleansing the air and adding a pop of green. Gardening on a larger scale takes you outdoors and into the open air, where you may enjoy birdsong, the wind on your face, the wonder of the sky, sunlight, and the benefits of vitamin D. Pondering the process of plant growth and marvelling at that of flowering does not fail to impress. For me, nothing is more satisfying than a day spent gardening, when at the end you can stand back and admire all you have achieved, feel connected to the earth and maybe eat something that you have grown.

Gardening with a friend, family members or helping a neighbour in need provides companionship and support, or in the realm of a community garden, strengthens bonds with those that live around us. Community gardens provide many benefits for participants, who may not otherwise have the space, knowledge or equipment. Community members have the opportunity to grow food, gather with a shared goal and a common purpose, to pool their knowledge, share their produce and interact socially. Through my involvement with Blairgowrie Community Garden I've experienced how much people benefit from this style of neighbourhood gardening, with impressive results.

Personally, for me the garden is a space where my imagination is stimulated and where possibilities are endless. I was seven years old when my mother died, and our garden was a reliable, safe retreat for me. Now in my fifties I still find comfort and joy in gardening, fiddling with plants and growing much of what we eat. It is a space in which I can lose myself, forget worries and find a sense of accomplishment in simple tasks. It is also a place where I can be creative, designing and planting new arrangements, moving potted plants around and picking foliage and flowers to display inside.

Professionally, my role as a landscape designer has been to design successful outdoor spaces for people in all types of settings and situations. But my role has never been solely clinical or practical: I encourage people to realise the benefits of being surrounded by plants and to engage with the natural world – for the good of all of us.

RIGHT Honeyeaters love the spectacular flowers of olive green *Phormium tenax,* rising from the roughly rendered blade walls. The staggered arrangement of these driveway walls on this steeply sloping site creates a range of microsites for a variety of plants.

ABOVE Drifts of *Poa labillardieri* and *Lomandra longifolia* 'Tanika' soften the zone between house and lake margins, with *Anigozanthos* 'Big Red' providing important summer colour. *Allocasuarina littoralis* frame the views of the water.

THE CREATION OF KARKALLA

Karkalla is on Bunurong country, land of the Kulin. The author acknowledges the deep and continuing connection that Traditional Owners have to these lands and waters and recognises their ongoing role in caring for Country.

BUILDING THE VISION

By the time I moved to Sorrento on Victoria's Mornington Peninsula, as a single woman again, I had gained enough confidence from landscaping experiments in Albury to try gravel gardening on a larger scale. Finding the right land took intensive searching and late in 1993 I bought an extraordinary 2-acre (8000 m²) property on a narrow part of the peninsula, with wide views south to Bass Strait and northwards to Port Phillip. The site was long, narrow and elevated in the centre with sandy hydrophobic soils. Most of the land was covered in declining coastal tea-tree (*Leptospermum laevigatum*), to about five metres in height, and a smorgasbord of weeds. *Pittosporum undulatum, Cotoneaster, Polygala* and a variety of ground weeds seemed to account for at least half the vegetation.

An original 1950s fibro shack sat on the highest part of the land. This I utilised as a studio/office while I became familiar with the land and thought deeply about the design and location of a new dwelling. Around this time I met, through a mutual friend, Sydney-based architect and builder Tom Isaksson. We quickly discovered that we shared a love of Modernist architecture, and before long I had engaged Tom to design and build a house with me. Work began in 1994.

The house was designed primarily with solar radiation in mind, maximising the winter exposure to the sun and minimising exposure to the cold prevailing winds from the ocean. We incorporated

LEFT 'Koonya Beach Columns' by Chris Booth are like beacons in the landscape. The species selection and arrangement of the gardened areas are designed to connect the garden proper with the bushland and ocean beyond.

solar-powered hot water, a composting toilet system called Rota-loo, rainfall collection, greywater recycling systems, and double glazing where it was most valuable. Other environmental considerations were investigated and adopted too: natural oil-based sealers and paints, sheep's wool insulation, re-using parts of the existing shack, and second-hand timbers for as many carpentry components as possible. I was fortunate to buy many metres of thick New Zealand kauri that had been used as floorboards in a warehouse in Flemington. We chose aluminium window and door frames for their durability in the harsh ocean-facing conditions and a copper roof and guttering that would never require replacing and with time acquire a beautiful verdigris. Over time we've also added solar panels that generate enough electricity for home use, and surplus to sell back to the grid.

One of the stand-out features of the design is the locally sourced limestone-clad feature walls, which run spine-like through the house and at intervals out into the landscape like buttresses, to form courtyards for wind protection and to anchor the house visually to the landscape. I had collected this stone for two years prior to building. Fortuitously, in 1994, while planning the house I met David Swann, a Melbourne-based landscape contractor who soon became my partner in love, life and work. We shared a love of skiing, hiking, gardening, the beach and the great outdoors and, unbeknown to us both, he had a natural talent for skilfully designing and building limestone walls – it was quite a match. Although limestone quarries no longer exist on the Mornington Peninsula, reefs of this white chalky stone are sometimes discovered during an excavation for a new house site or swimming pool and can be purchased from the builder. I wanted the materiality of our new home to relate strongly in character to the site and indeed its ocean location, creating a strong sense of place.

We wanted to tread as lightly as possible on the unique site by respecting and working with what it had to offer, both from a house and landscape perspective. Hand in hand with the design of the house came garden ideas and concepts. As we spent more and more time on site building, we came to understand much more about the site conditions and could think through how the garden spaces could best work.

The house was designed in a wide U shape with the opening of the U facing south, screened and protected by old stands of *Leptospermum laevigatum*. This sunken courtyard space is sheltered from every direction and when the hot north wind howls it is a calm place to retreat to. The apex of the building's U is to the north with views towards Port Phillip. This upper area is terraced and is protected from the west wind by a limestone wall which flanks that side. This wall also shields the view of the arrival forecourt where cars park, and it continues internally to form the backdrop to the fireplace. There is always an advantage in conceiving the house design in conjunction

ABOVE Clipping and sculpting of many Australian native plants signals intent and gives shape to species which may otherwise look unkept in a domestic garden setting. It is also rejuvenating – like any other form of tip pruning – and can increase the amount of light getting through by judicious tidying of the canopy and trunks.

ABOVE Seas of fine granitic gravel draw us through the garden and negate the need for garden beds. The oversized limestone feature and large balls of *Alyxia buxifolia* subtly cue a transition to the natural bushland and partially obscure what's beyond.

with the garden concept as it marries them strongly; at Karkalla – named after the native succulent which is rampant across the property – it is difficult to distinguish where one finishes and the other begins. The repeated use of natural materials such as the limestone and complementary textures and colours inside, outside and in the transitions reinforces this union.

Karkalla sits among the tertiary dunes – the third dune back from the beach, covered in what is classified as alkaline scrub. It is far enough away from the ocean to be protected from direct sea spray but not immune to the effects of a marine environment in terms of corrosion. Since I had no experience living so close to the coast some trial and error was involved when it came to plant selection and subsequent success. I spent a lot of time exploring and walking along the nearby Mornington Peninsula National Park tracks, observing what indigenous species grew where so I could select and habitat match within our own garden. This fieldwork, plus research into species from Mediterranean climates, ultimately formed the basis of my plant selection. Other than the areas set aside for food production, I wanted to choose plants that would not require artificial irrigation beyond the establishment phase. To give them the best possible start, using small plant stock and planting at the optimum time of the year – autumn and winter – was advantageous, as was mulching, vigilant weed control and occasional supplementary irrigation during the warmer and drier months.

Among the local species that I had admired thriving in the national park behind Karkalla were drooping she-oak (*Allocasuarina verticillata*), sweet bursaria (*Bursaria spinulosa*), karkalla or pigface (*Carpobrotus rossii*), white correa (*Correa alba*), native fuschia (*C. reflexa*), coast banksia (*Banksia integrifolia*), moonah (*Melaleuca lanceolata*), cushion bush (*Leucophyta brownii*), knobby club rush (*Ficinia nodosa*), coastal daisybush (*Olearia axillaris*), coastal speargrass (*Austrostipa stipoides*), mat rush (*Lomandra longifolia*) and coast everlasting (*Ozothamnus turbinatus*). Frustratingly, not all species that I wanted to plant were available from nurseries at that time, however I procured and planted a large variety and quantity nonetheless. I designed the arrangement of these species in the garden in a style that was less haphazard than observed in nature to distinguish it from the bush beyond – but not too much. More species became available, and in larger sizes, when I started working with local propagators and nurseries. Introduced species included olives (*Olea europaea*) to provide a structural framework on the front terrace and frame the views, as well as pride of Madeira (*Echium candicans*), various types of phormium and cordyline, euphorbia, aeonium, cotyledon, senecio, hebe, santolina, lavender and statice.

Looking back, there was a lot of variety in my initial planting – maybe too much to create a cohesive look; however, with time nature

MY JOURNEY WITH PLANTS

LEFT The arrangement of plants, hardscaping elements such as terrace walls, furniture and decorative items requires careful consideration for it to fulfil intent but remain casual. Planting and pruning in this gravelled courtyard mimics nature's slightly random groupings observed in the nearby national park.

41

took care of this. Plants that died were generally not replaced with the same and those that didn't thrive were either moved or removed. Anything that thrived that I liked, and which served a purpose, was repeated and a more cohesive picture began to form. Falling into the trap of too much variety happens frequently when designing planting schemes, especially in home garden situations. Plant temptation is everywhere, but if you are not careful, initial declarations of a thoughtfully designed scheme can be derailed. Setting tight parameters – and sticking to them – as well as accepting the process of natural attrition are useful brakes on confusion and excess in your garden.

The large terrace on the north side and the courtyard on the south side of the house were built on what was essentially pure sand, and on top of this we laid a 180–200 mm layer of local crushed granite gravel base. We planted straight into the gravel, then compacted this layer with a whacker, finally spreading a thin layer of 5–7 mm of crushed granite, known as crusher dust, as a final mulch. Once this was completed it was time to wait and see how the various plants handled the gravel mulch. I was fairly confident about the survival rate of most of the species since I had observed many of them growing in similar conditions. Gravel road shoulders, *en tout cas* tennis courts and coarse sand and gravel terraces in the nearby national park all appeared to provide a very similar medium. We did not create garden beds or use topsoil and compost but rather added a small handful of pelletised chicken manure to each planting hole.

I had topped the plantings with granitic gravel mulch, not only to supply additional nutrients and minerals but also to conserve moisture. I had seen this type of growing situation in Beth Chatto's garden in the UK and while hiking at Mount Buffalo National Park and Wilsons Promontory, where plants were thriving in coarse granitic gravels. This approach had also been trialled in our Albury garden. I noted that many of these species in their natural habitats would shrink and really struggle during the drying summer months; however, in my newly created garden many plants behaved quite differently. I had *Carpobrotus rossii* advancing across the seas of gravel, *Leucophyta brownii* as big as small cars in the rear courtyard, *Correa alba* specimens with long leggy arms and *Ficinia nodosa* self-sowing with abandon. I had a plant riot on my hands.

In an attempt to emulate the salt-laden strong winds of Bass Strait I reached for the hedge shears and went to work on the shrubs. Most shrubs and trees growing on the windward cliff faces and dunes were being sheared and shaped naturally by wind and in some cases wallabies. In my domain I needed to act as these forces. I soon had the unruly plants in hand. To my surprise, there was one species in particular that did not enjoy my severe pruning: *Olearia axillaris*. Each specimen soon developed a rust fungus and quickly died. I concluded

ABOVE Multiple stems of *Melaleuca lanceolata* have been clipped into a single dome, revealing shapely trunks and the opportunity to see through to an upper level. The blond bombshell *Austrostipa stipoides* ties in through tone and habit with the granitic gravel and limestone walls. A stand of *Banksia integrifolia* provides year-round habitat for bird and insect life.

that it did not enjoy having the amount of air circulating through its centre altered. I learnt to prune it as I prune rosemary, by removing up to a third of its growth each year by cutting into the shrub as opposed to trimming it into a ball. This way you can enjoy its branch arrangement and natural habit while simultaneously rejuvenating it and keeping it tidy.

Leucophyta brownii is one of those odd characters that took me some time to understand. Observing it growing in the dunes near our house, I noticed that the plant's open, twiggy habit would fill with sand, leaving the fresh new grey growth visible. The sand obscured its unsightly dead-looking lower branches. In a garden situation, without the sandy infill, it grows quickly and easily but I have found it to be too short-lived and for that reason I rarely use it in gardens we design. At home, it happily self-seeds in nooks and crannies of the gravel terraces and is in a continual process of replacement.

Needless to say, I was on a steep learning curve in my early days at Karkalla, learning about the conditions favoured by all the new additions. I was enjoying the challenges enormously and was encouraged by many of the results.

PAGE BEFORE Plants of different heights and foliage are used to blur the boundary between gardened areas and the native coastal plantings beyond. Carefully assess the character and scale of plants needed to aid that transition. *Westringia fruticosa* (centre) is easy to shape and grows readily in this seaside habitat.

ABOVE Offset walls with openings, not gates, encourage movement through the garden, as do points of interest like sculptures and feature plants.

ABOVE Karkalla's living room opens to the north-facing terrace. The house is linked to the landscape by the spine of limestone wall and the continuous concrete bench. The use of colours common to both inside and out reinforces this marriage.

THE CREATION OF KARKALLA

KITCHEN GARDENS, ORCHARD AND PLANTING

One of my long-held dreams in the 1990s was to grow a substantial amount of what my family and I ate, at least in terms of fruit, vegetables, herbs and eggs. It was important to me that we could always prepare a fresh and simple meal from what we grew, to know where that produce had been grown and how it had been grown. Now with 2 acres of land, and with much of it sheltered and sunny, I had the opportunity to put my horticultural skills and understanding of permaculture practices into action.

Fortunately, we had a protected, low-lying area which largely fit the bill for an orchard. It was covered in dead or failing *Leptospermum laevigatum*, which we were able to legally remove. This area also offered the deepest topsoil, still a mere 150 mm; not deep or particularly rich by most standards, it was better than beginning with nothing. The pH of the soil was neutral – but too high for healthy fruit trees – and we went about the massive task of decreasing the pH by increasing the humus in the soil. Initially, truckloads of chicken manure were bought from a local organic poultry farmer and many forms of organic matter, such as seaweed and lucerne hay were layered over the surface. Fruit trees were then selected; I chose some cultivars that I knew would thrive – I'd seen them doing so in my neighbours' gardens – and others were a gamble. Apricots, almonds, plums, peaches, pomegranates, cherries, nectarines, apples, pears, quinces and figs all stood a good chance. Others I chose were suitable for our frost-free coastal location and would be well suited for the amphitheatre-like site that trapped the sun's warmth. These included macadamia nut, a custard apple I was assured would grow this far south, and other subtropical species. Sadly, citrus of every type and cultivar have never succeeded for us. Despite constant spoiling with compost, water and warmth the combination of sandy soils and coolish summers do not equal abundant fruit nor healthy looking trees at Karkalla. The neutral pH means that available iron is not readily absorbed by tree roots and as a result citrus particularly become iron deficient.

We chose a flattish area of land between the orchard and existing chook house to establish the kitchen garden. The chook house and run had been built by the previous owners – who remain our neighbours – and we decided early on to leave it in situ and share in

LEFT *Cotyledon* and *aeonium*, with their fleshy rosettes and quirky stems, combined with
Phormium tenax reflect the early morning light and connect the scene to the bay view beyond.
Old timber steps lead down to the garden/chook shed, kitchen garden and orchard.

51

ABOVE Celery, fennel, spring onions, radicchio and varieties of heirloom lettuce are often left to self-seed – as free recruits and fodder for birds and insects.

the care of the chooks and eggs: a perfect communal arrangement that suited both households.

While the house was being built, I had purchased many tonnes of old pier timbers from the Portsea pier renovation. We used these richly aged beams of mainly yellow box timber and built an elevated timber kitchen garden with a crisscrossing of paths in a beautifully symmetrical design. With the infill of veggies and herbs it was like a giant jewel-studded star. Compost bins were fashioned from the same pier timbers and a fence made from recycled tobacco drying sticks from north-eastern Victoria installed around the perimeter. We were up and running finally.

There was enough room for an enormous bed of my beloved dahlias within the fenced garden. Dahlias were a childhood favourite of mine and had been grown passionately by our elderly housekeeper. For Andy, the bigger the better; she would diligently use her old pantyhose to secure the large floppy blooms to tomato stakes or old broom handles. I grew them in memory of Andy and her upcycling ways. Dahlias are perfect to grow in free-draining sandy soil since they do not require lifting in winter to prevent the rotting of their tubers. They provide extravagantly coloured flowers, beautiful in a vase or bouquet, from Christmas to April. With time my collection expanded and now contains many from the French Delbard collection, bred especially for hot and sunny conditions such as ours. I find the showy blooms – with delicious names such as Pondicherry, Soleil Couchant, Versailles, Mont Blanc, Cheverny and Napoleon – irresistible and I am forever adding more to the garden, with happy results. Many a tuber has been shared with gardening friends. Outside the kitchen garden and adjacent orchard, restraint of colour returns.

Although I had not been able to lay out the garden areas according to permaculture zones exactly, I was basically following a zone 1 and zone 2 arrangement. The biggest digression was that I was unable to position zone 1 around or adjacent to the house since it was too windy and the soil unsuitable for growing food. My zone 1 sat further to the north and in a lower and sheltered position with the daily jobs of attending to the chooks, emptying the compost bucket, and harvesting vegetables and herbs all conveniently together. Closer to the kitchen I was able to establish a hardy herb collection beneath the clothes line where I could conveniently grab a handful of seasoning. Beyond zone 1 we had positioned zone 2 which contained the orchard and was close to the front gate where we could have lucerne hay and manures delivered with ease. Today our beehives are positioned in the orchard, where they help in the pollination of fruit trees, vegetables and other plants.

Once the planned garden spaces of kitchen garden, orchard, house terraces and courtyards immediately surrounding the house were built, planted and growing, our attention turned to the remaining acre and a half. This area was a mix of *Leptospermum laevigatum* interspersed with woody weed species. Herbaceous weeds included *Dipogon lignosus,* which crawled over nearly everything, *Smilax,* and *Panicum,* its seeds remaining viable for some seven years.

Most of the naturally occurring vegetation likely to have been growing had been cleared by the late 1880s to quarry and burn lime. What we were dealing with was a predominantly disturbed site that was now covered with a new mix of species. Our overall aim was to remove the woody weeds, whipper snip the panic grasses and then mulch as much of the area as we had energy and time to do. As each area was tackled, indigenous tube stock and larger plants were planted. I chose new plantings depending on what indigenous species remained in each area, the amount of shelter and shade present combined with the look I wanted to achieve.

Planting a diversity of species was an important consideration too. Fortunately, there were two local nursery people at this time who understood the importance of local provenance and only used propagation material, both seeds and cuttings, collected from the southern end of the peninsula. This gave the newly planted selections the best chance of survival and ensured a continuum of species whose genetics were local. This revegetation, as many will appreciate, took a lot of work. Clearing, weeding, mulching, planting and watering were all ongoing tasks that took much of our time. Fortunately, 'plant guarding' of the new plantings was not required since we had a rabbit-proof fence installed around the perimeter of the property early on.

This approach did not go unrewarded. With time the species of birds in the garden increased, echidnas appeared, and various small reptiles like blue-tongue lizards, skinks and snakes all began to make their presence felt. Insect life flourished too. The rewilding of the bulk of the block was successful and the proliferation in numbers of these animal species proved it. We also noticed that a dormant bank of seeds belonging to local plant species would often germinate in just-cleared areas, especially if it was an open space. Accordingly, we adjusted our mulching regime to be selective rather than broad so we could see what appeared naturally and encourage what we wanted.

Our first daughter Ella was born in 1998, and we were excited by how delighted she was watching bird and animal life around the garden, collecting chook eggs, and helping us in the kitchen garden with her own tools. A long-held dream was finally being realised and we couldn't have been happier.

By the time the garden was four years old, it was beginning to look reasonably established and make pictures of its own. I was thrilled by many of the plant successes and by the way the house and landscape had begun to merge and feel like they belonged to one

ABOVE Small-weave netting protects a quince tree and most other
fruit trees in the orchard against rat, bird and possum raids.

another. I was also very pleased with my gravel gardening attempts as I now had beautiful and successful examples of this method of gardening to show prospective clients. The term 'gravel gardening' does not conjure up images of great beauty for most people but now I could demonstrate – they could see for themselves – how easy and successful this approach was.

In 2000 the garden came to the attention of *The Age*'s garden writer Sarah Guest, who was working on a book with garden photographer Simon Griffiths called *Gardens in Australia*. I knew Sarah very well and she admired my newly designed and planted garden. She also understood how difficult it could be to establish a successful garden in this sort of demanding location since she gardened on a hilltop in nearby Blairgowrie. Sarah and the publisher decided to feature Karkalla and use a photograph of our front terrace on the cover. Naturally, we were thrilled. She included a chapter on the garden called 'Modernist' and wrote: 'The garden is about space, sculpture and place – its own'. For me, this was an enormous compliment and it helped to open people's eyes to what I was achieving in a garden design realm.

Many people have trouble visualising ideas, especially newish ones like gravel gardening was then, and the book's beautiful photographs of Karkalla helped readers begin to understand this application. When you mention the word 'gravel' many people immediately think of a rough gravel road or possibly something agricultural. They do not picture gentle seas of wheat-coloured gravel that travel under plants, connecting the open spaces with the planted areas without interruption. It has a seamless quality that makes the garden scene restful and expansive. It is similar to a lawn in this way – without the edging, mowing and watering.

Connecting the more planned areas of the garden with the surrounding revegetation areas was something that I considered carefully. I did not want there to be an obvious delineation between what we had designed and planted around the house with the areas of revegetation we had established among what was naturally occurring. There were many species common to both areas but laid out in different ways and maintained differently too. In the more planned areas, these species were planted in groupings, and drifts and shrub species were clipped into tight shapes as they grew. Some tree species also suffered the indignity of being tortured into lollipops (*Allocasuarina verticillata*) and mushrooms on multiple legs or giant balls (*Melaleuca lanceolata*). In the revegetated bush areas these plants were more carelessly placed – the only considerations being suitability to a particular niche and the views from the house and through the landscape. As these revegetation plants grew, the shrubs were occasionally clipped to increase bushiness but not to the same extent as the more 'gardened'

LEFT A retaining wall from reclaimed pier timbers with groupings of clipped shrubs and pruned olive trees of varying heights define a gravel path, softened by rosemary and a clump of flowering *Lomandra longifolia*. The feel is decidedly Mediterranean hillside.

areas. As the eye moved away from the 'house gardens' the planting loosened up and began to integrate with the relaxed bush setting and the national park beyond: we were blurring the boundaries between where the garden proper ceased and the bush beyond began.

In 2002 we welcomed our second daughter Yasmin into our lives and our young family required additions and adaptations to the garden. A simple tea-tree picket fence was installed across the front of the terrace to prevent Ella lowering herself off this high shelf, and the succulent plantings that were brittle to the knock of balls and bikes were replaced with more hardy tussocks and shrubs. We wanted our girls to be able to use and explore the garden spaces without being reprimanded or limited. A cubby house was initiated and became a project that David and the girls spent hours building together from materials left over from landscaping jobs or salvaged from the local tip. Later an in-ground trampoline was installed and my childhood jungle gym brought over from my sister's home. It was becoming a garden for our girls and their friends to explore and create in.

With time other additions were necessary too. A small bungalow was built for friends and family to use and a playroom for the girls built onto the side of the house. Alongside the necessary physical expansions came the addition of pieces of garden sculpture both designed and found. New plants were added for trialling or to replace areas of dead *Leptospermum laevigatum*.

One of the most recent changes has been the design and establishment of a new terrace tucked into the northern slope beneath the front of the house. This area is out of reach of the prevailing winds and receives the maximum amount of solar radiation which we delight in during the colder months. David installed a woodfired oven at one end of this terrace, behind another of his beautifully crafted limestone walls, with an opening and shelf in the middle to access the oven from. It is an area for star and moon gazing by a fire pit, for cooking using our garden's bounty and dining with friends in a warm and sheltered situation; you feel held by the landscape.

In addition to this terrace, on the slope below came another opportunity to grow more food and provide fodder for our bees. Rows of rosemary and English lavender have been established and in between these we plant sunflowers for summer picking and larger vegetables. Rows of garlic, brassicas, tomatoes, peppers and eggplants now supply even more of our vegetable requirements.

The Karkalla garden is constantly evolving, speckled with disappointments, surprises, triumphs and a variety of lessons for all. It is shared with friends, family and neighbourhood visitors feathered, furred and human. It is, after all, the process of gardening which is so rewarding and not necessarily the end result.

ABOVE Dahlias thrive in the kitchen garden's raised perimeter beds, where they are easy to admire and convenient to pick on the way to some salad greens. Spent sunflower heads are left for seed-eating birds and often as supports for other plants.

MY JOURNEY WITH PLANTS

ABOVE The fenced kitchen garden is a multifunction space, positioned on the site's only relatively level, sunny and protected area. Compost bays are by the gate, within easy barrow distance of the beds and orchard.

GARDEN DESIGN

UNDERSTANDING
THE SITE

ABOVE Careful consideration of a site's character early in the design process is imperative for developing a strong sense of place that makes the most of the site's assets. In some situations it may be necessary to undertake an inward focus, with screening and greening, to create a sanctuary.

Understanding indicators is at the heart of a thorough site investigation. Approach a potential garden site as an investigator would, searching for clues which will inform you of the nature of the site and its peculiarities.

If available, make a copy of any site survey or information provided by the client or real estate agent. If a features and levels survey is not available a surveyor can be engaged to prepare this important document as a starting point. This to-scale document accurately records any site features that are visible – powerlines and poles, significant vegetation, built structures including the positions of site services, drains, windows and doors – and can be commissioned by the landscape designer, architect or homeowner. Otherwise, make some rough to-scale sketches, noting site orientation, house site, key features, fences and your initial thoughts on vistas and views – good and bad. I take smartphone photos of any visual pointers, make notes and scribble extensively on the survey if existing. Be prepared to revise and revisit numerous times; I visit during different weather events if I think it will be revealing.

It's important to begin your analysis before you even set foot on site: I like to approach a site slowly on my initial visit, eyes open to the topography and surrounds. Note the orientation of the site and pay attention to what is around it. In the preliminary phase of the project, it is critical to visit the site at different times of the day to observe the path of the sun and its effects on the site. Shade cast from neighbouring buildings, vegetation or a landmass will directly affect how much light falls – or does not – on different parts of the site. Visiting in the evening or at night can provide information about potential light pollution and traffic noise at peak hour.

ABOVE *Bambusa multiplex* 'Goldstripe' and *Parthenocissus quinquefolia* soften the streetscape. Species were selected to cope with root competition from the large neighbouring eucalypt – a recognised plus and minus of the site.

RIGHT Ocean-facing gardens confront pummeling winds, and gardeners shouldn't pretend otherwise. A considered site assessment may reveal options for creating windbreaks or utilising more protected spaces on site.

Try to read the character of the surrounding landscape. Adjacent vegetation, whether it be naturally occurring or introduced, and current land uses can provide valuable information about likely soil type and prevailing wind direction and strength. Stony or rocky outcrops may be apparent and will tell you more about soil type, and depth to some extent. It's easy to look past weeds, or plants growing out of place, but their presence tells you something. The occurrence of certain weeds can indicate conditions such as mineral and nutrient deficiencies in the soil, salinity, compaction and waterlog. I recommend making a list of all the weeds present – or take photos – and research later what they indicate about the soil or conditions. Digging holes in various locations across the site will also give further information about the soil properties.

Likewise, as you're scouting for weeds, look for the presence of animal scats – from rabbits, possums and other Australian marsupials such as wombats or kangaroos – which foretells some of the challenges you may face in establishing new plantings. Plant guards and exclusion fencing may well be required to protect your tender young plants if the problem looks challenging.

Other critical information such as average rainfall and distribution can be gathered online, or from the client, especially in rural locations, where rainfall records are often obsessively kept, accounting for any seasonal variations.

Just as important as site assessment is client assessment. If you are designing a domestic garden space this is most effectively done at the client's home when all parties are present. 'My partner is not interested in the garden' may be the case during the design phase but can change rapidly at the invoicing phase. Most parties do have ideas and preferences about a potential garden given an opportunity to contribute. 'I'd love a lemon tree for a G&T' or 'I don't want it to be a lot of work', and from many younger participants: 'Can we have a water slide?'

A brief from the client is imperative, telling you of their desired inclusions, tastes and budget; however, the firsthand observation of someone's home tells you a lot about their character, lifestyle and expectations. Are they untidy? Neat? Are their interiors bright? Subdued? Cluttered? Restful? Seeing clients in their own space is very useful when it comes to building a profile of them. I don't request a formal Q&A style brief but like to chat with potential clients about expectations and inclusions and jot down notes as we go. A more formal list of inclusions is presented in the fee proposal and the client will then see on the concept plan exactly what will be included.

In addition to a brief from the client, it is critical to tease out and understand what style of landscape they envisage or want to experience. I find it especially useful to draw them out on how they would like to *feel* in various landscape spaces and what they like about a particular garden style. It might be the pared-back simplicity of a Japanese garden, the looseness or variety of a cottage garden, or a sheltered sun trap like a Mediterranean courtyard. Taking clients to visit past projects provides an opportunity to gauge their reaction to different landscape spaces. Providing photographs of established gardens is also useful if it is not possible to take a client to a particular garden. It is essential to identify what will make a client feel comfortable and pleased with their own new landscape. One person's idea of a wild romantic landscape is another person's idea of an overgrown mess.

All of this gathered information, together with the client brief and the visual observations made during site assessment form what's called a site profile. At this point, design ideas begin to form around style and arrangement of components.

With many of my domestic garden projects – where space permits – I extol the virtues of growing some of your own produce. If a client reports they buy lemons from the supermarket I encourage them to plant a trusty citrus, explaining how the evergreen, bushy lemon tree could do double-duty by screening an unsightly element, like the neighbour's shed. I admit I struggle to connect with clients who want no more than an easy-to-look-after or 'Whatever you think we should have' type of garden. Gardens can give people so much more than that, and I believe it is part of my role to show them what a well thought out garden can deliver. I want people to feel invested in their new garden and be actively involved in what it will contain and look like. With time, seeing clients enjoying their outside spaces and hearing how much time they spend using them is what gives me the reward of fulfilment and job satisfaction.

ABOVE Drifts of *Poa poiformis* and groupings of native shrubs mark the end of this garden and the beginning of the bushland beyond.

ABOVE *Leptospermum laevigatum* and *Allocasuarina verticillata* are pruned each year to form an overhead canopy and maintain space for vehicles to travel easily along the driveway of undulations, reminiscent of the nearby dunes.

69

SENSE OF PLACE

Sense of place refers to our relationship with a place or site and the sense of belonging or connecting to it. It's important because it makes you feel comfortable in a garden space and fosters the sense of something being just right. In a landscape realm, sense of place refers to a particular characteristic (or set) that makes the site unique. This may be intrinsic, or it may be understood from looking at the past use of the site. Research may be necessary to gather information about a site and its context – historical, industrial or ecological, for example – to help develop a sense of place. Reading a site to obtain cues is not always about the visual observation of materials and plants, as it can also be about sounds and scents. The salty breeze, sounds of crashing waves, the line of a river or creek, birdlife in nearby trees, or wind racing through the canopy are very evocative sensory experiences that may be utilised in developing sense of place.

The use of locally sourced hard landscaping materials in a garden design is an obvious and reliable approach to reinforcing a sense of place. Selecting appropriate plant species, especially those indigenous to a particular site or area, can also connect you to a garden space. Introduced plant species in nearby landscapes can also fulfil this role. For example, a design for a new garden in an area known for its brilliant autumn foliage could incorporate similar species for their display and create a sense of connection or belonging to that town and area.

Replicating a species from the surrounds within a new garden is not always appropriate in terms of scale or horticultural suitability but a planting idea can be reinterpreted. Seas of yellowed tussocks in a paddock could be replicated in a garden setting using a species that has better longevity or more pleasing year-round appearance. Plants can be pruned to special effect as well, mimicking nature. Shrubs and trees clipped into wind-sheared shapes are reminiscent of those discovered on seaside rambles, and other bushland elements can be re-created in a garden setting using found material.

ABOVE Retain suitable local species – especially trees – that are repeated in the surrounding landscape. Planting on this site is staggered down the slope, effectively absorbing and framing the pastureland view.

ABOVE This contemporary walled kitchen garden is connected to the coastal landscape through the palette of materials selected, including local grey gravel, weathered timber battens, off-form concrete walls and carefully chosen plant species to reinforce a sense of belonging.

71

ABOVE Bay views wrap around an ancient, carefully manicured *Melaleuca lanceolata*. Planting is mostly indigenous, modest and low, to retain the water views and allow the moonah to feature.

BELOW Formal hedging of *Murraya paniculata* mirrors the clean, modern lines of this inner-city, multi-level home. *Jacaranda mimosifolia* and deciduous *Lagerstroemia* trees will balance the front façade over time, with restrained spacing.

Developing a sense of place in an urban setting can sometimes be a more challenging task. There are not always views of borrowed landscape that are desirable, and sadly many of the borrowed views in cities and towns are of elements which require screening rather than inclusion. As a result, domestic landscapes in urban situations are often inward looking and interest needs to be designed and developed within the confines of the boundaries. It may be that you need to concentrate on hard landscape materials which complement the urban setting in this instance: metals, concrete, bluestone cobble, rusted industrial material.

Developing sense of place using foliage matching in an urban environment is a tool that can be used to advantage when considering the garden proper in relation to the broader landscape. It may not be possible to repeat exact species, due to size limitations or differences in growing conditions, but it is possible to adopt colours, textures and shapes from the view beyond. On the Mornington Peninsula, *Melaleuca lanceolata*, *Allocasuarina verticillata*, *Leptospermum laevigatum* and *Banksia integrifolia* are the dominant indigenous tree species. At Karkalla we have repeated these species within the garden boundaries to visually connect with the surrounding landscape. For the same effect in a smaller garden, I would repeat plants with similar form, leaf texture or colour to those in the surrounding landscape.

In a design for a rooftop terrace in St Kilda I used clipped domes of *Buxus sempervirens* for their similar shape and colour to reference the large dome-shaped *Ulmus procera* in view in the nearby parkland. The voluminous grass species *Miscanthus transmorrisonensis* connected the roof terrace to the yellow and blond tones found in the autumn foliage of the receding canopy.

Introducing an artwork, sculpture or material elements that reflect the garden's location – think reclaimed historic timbers, local rock and stone or industrial relics – can reinforce a sense of belonging. For Karkalla, we commissioned a piece made from local limestone and Western District sandstone (see page 103 for more on sculpture as features).

Links can also be made through colour. The sea-blue colour of the canvas in the sun loungers on the terrace connect the garden of Karkalla to the blue of the bay beyond. Indoor colour schemes can visually connect that space with plantings outside in similar or complementary tones. In our Melbourne garden we laid bright grass-green carpet in the two front rooms that overlook the park opposite, and this connects us visually to this green expanse.

Of all garden design techniques, repetition is one of the most effective. The repetition of colour, form and texture is a tool that can be employed in many situations to reinforce the connection between situations and develop sense of place for a landscape.

CHOOSING PLANTS THAT FLOURISH

Using locally indigenous plants in landscape design has many advantages. The plants that have evolved in a particular region are far more likely to thrive in a new garden being established in the same area than many introduced species. Local plants are most able to cope with the given circumstances – soil type and depth, rainfall, temperatures, frost, wind, salt spray – and will require fewer artificial inputs to ensure success. But a plant list does not have to be exclusively indigenous species, and if you choose plants wisely from regions with a similar climate and soil to your own they will also thrive. Plants with similar origins will have evolved within similar parameters and are likely to require less site preparation and coddling. Be aware that these plants are also potential weeds.

Ecological matching as an approach to successful plant establishment is extremely useful but also potentially devastating. Gardeners must take responsible ownership of some species. I am careful not to use species that too readily self-seed and may potentially naturalise in a nearby area of bush or national park. *Agapanthus orientalis* from South Africa, *Billardiera heterophylla* syn. *Sollya heterophylla* from Western Australia and *Pittosporum undulatum* from New South Wales and Queensland are just three species that have naturalised in our area. It is important to research where potential garden inclusions originate from and if they come from an area with a similar climate or set of circumstances proceed with caution and respect.

Many of the indigenous plant species on the Mornington Peninsula and other coastal areas have small leathery leaves. This is a survival advantage because these plants have evolved to cope with harsh, salt-laden winds; alkaline, sandy soils and periods of drought. The colour and leaf size does not vary all that much, so I find it useful in some gardens to supplement the plant palette with species from other parts of Australia and the world. Depending on the style of planting sought I may add larger-leaved feature plants like phormium, cordyline, miscanthus and *Tetrapanax papyrifer*. The flower size and colour of the local indigenous species are generally quite subdued, and this may be enhanced with

LEFT Sculptural *Melaleuca armillaris* retained from the original garden is underplanted with *Phormium tenax* 'Anna Red', softly rounded *Westringia fruticosa* and low-growing *Correa reflexa* var. *nummulariifolia*, a useful spreading plant with lime green bells in winter.

the addition of aloe, limonium, alyogyne, echium, euphorbia and buddleja that have brighter, larger flowers. Some of these species have the ability to freely self-seed in the sandy soils of Mornington Peninsula so we are very careful to remove spent flower heads before potential plant naturalisation occurs.

I believe it is important to be guided by the site parameters in choosing a plant palette rather than attempting to change the site to include a particular plant story. For example, it would be madness to attempt to grow cooler–climate loving azalea, camellia, cornus and magnolia, which require acid-rich soils and shelter, on an exposed dune of neutral hydrophobic sand.

The development of a particular garden style or theme, such as cottage or Japanese, can be achieved successfully with this in mind. It is a matter of selecting species that are matched to the site parameters and exhibit characteristics that can deliver a particular theme. For example, the Japanese *Pinus thunbergii* could be replaced with *Leucopogon parviflorus* in a coastal setting and pruned in a similar way. Then it is the arrangement of plants in the planting palette that completes the rest of the picture.

RIGHT *Betula utilis* var. *jacquemontii*, *Bartlettina sordida* and *Liriope muscari* 'Evergreen Giant' thrive on this shaded side of the house, where heavy soils and excess water are a challenge.

ABOVE *Austrostipa stipoides* and silver-leaved *Leucophyta brownii* are indigenous to south-east Australia's coast and cover the dunes and limestone cliffs of the southern end of the Mornington Peninsula.

RIGHT A favourite at Karkalla, *Austrostipa stipoides* is a useful choice for its golden heads and the beautiful way it moves in the wind, patterning the gravel with gentle sweeps.

RETAINED AND REPURPOSED MATERIALS

For me, a garden is richer if it incorporates retained, recycled and repurposed elements. It appeals to me aesthetically and creatively but also makes sense environmentally. My design work is about forging relationships with our stunning and uniquely Australian landscapes and from my earliest days of practice I've preferred to use local materials and local plants, and aimed to step as lightly as possible on the land.

I was raised by a resourceful father, from the interwar generation, who instilled in my siblings and me the value of recycling, saving, re-using in the home and the garden – waste not, want not. We composted, mended, fixed, repurposed, passed on and used a thing to death. As much as we children often railed against it then, this approach to more sustainable, less wasteful living has seeped into many aspects of our life today and it can easily be applied to garden design in so many ways.

RETAIN

Keeping elements of the existing garden to re-use in the new one is an intrinsically rewarding and non-wasteful practice but also a tangible way to link the original garden or site with the new. Such a nod to the past could be retaining elements of the original garden structure or existing vegetation, re-using old bricks and slate from a path in a new structure – a terrace or patio – or using naturally occurring stone found during excavation.

LEFT Repurposed aged timbers, in this case from the Portsea pier, are available from local networks and can work well in low walls, steps or path inserts. They add an instant patina and reinforce local character.

ABOVE Solar panels and rainwater tanks installed at Karkalla to improve sustainability. The garden areas that are irrigated rely on collected rainwater and the household runs solely on solar-generated electricity.

RECYCLE

Many of us love the expressive 'patina of the old' found in recycled materials and it is useful to give an aged look to a new garden. Years ago, we came across hardwood timber battens, from the decommissioned Portland abattoirs, and bought thousands of them. They are a neutral weathered grey and a useful size and length for creating screens in a landscape. We use them extensively in our designs and they have become somewhat of a signature of ours.

Salvaged treasures like Hills Hoist rotary clothes lines, concrete laundry troughs, cast-iron baths, weathered and barnacled timbers from local piers and cleaned second-hand bricks have also made their way into our designs.

While recycling and upcycling can be a satisfying process, visually and economically, it is not always worthwhile. For example, it is not usually worth lifting old slate that is still strongly adhered to a concrete slab. Too much of the slate tends to break in the process and it can yield a disappointing result. Cleaning and re-using old bricks and honeycomb landscape rocks will achieve far better results.

ABOVE Nasturtiums clamber over a simple fence made of hardwood stakes, once used to dry tobacco in sheds in the north-east of Victoria, and form a textured backdrop for the prolifically blooming dahlias.

RIGHT Locally sourced feature rocks, granitic gravel and Australian plant species combine to create a restful garden that feels like it belongs to the landscape.

LOW-MILE MATERIALS

I prefer to use locally available materials whenever I can, as often as I can, in my designs. This is not only to minimise the energy footprint of the garden – through fewer miles travelled – but to actively choose ethically sourced and environmentally sustainable products. In Victoria, we are fortunate to be able to source and buy excellent quality stone that is extracted from Victorian quarries, such as slate from the Pyrenees, bluestone from the Western District and granite from the Mornington Peninsula. It is also important to consider the origin of timber used in landscaping as not all species are ethically or sustainably sourced. If I am unfamiliar with a species of timber or its origin, I ask the supplier where it comes from and carry out some research too. Fortunately, there are many sustainably harvested local and recycled options for timber these days and using a second-hand timber product can give a garden an instant patina and sense of belonging. Reclaimed timbers are often available in larger sizes than those made from newly felled and milled trees.

Local natural materials in a garden or site are also without peer when it comes to developing a sense of belonging to that place. Stone, rock and gravel are my 'hard' building materials of choice and I'm lucky to have excellent supplies nearby. On the southern end of the Mornington Peninsula limestone is the naturally occurring stone and it was used in many early Victorian buildings. Lime kilns were plentiful along the coast, burning lime for booming Melbourne construction in the 1880s. Traces of the kilns and limestone rubble walking paths are still evident in the area today. Over time, in this part of the country, limestone enters your subconscious as the material that looks at home and is indeed at home.

When I lived in Albury and first started designing, I sometimes worked on country properties, where my engagement to design and build new garden elements often extended well beyond the garden gates and into the paddocks. Farmers are resourceful people and I tried to be so too in my recommendations, recycling what I could but also keeping my eyes open for a plentiful local resource to be used in another way. One client's property near Lake Mokoan, north of Benalla, had abundant soft-pink granite outcrops on the farm, which we had crushed at a local plant to create gravel for paths and the driveway surfaces. This married the garden proper to the weathered rocks in the paddocks. Also emblematic of the site was the local river red gum, *Eucalyptus camaldulensis*, with a particularly creamy yellow smooth bark. We collected seed to produce offspring perfectly adapted to the given conditions for use in shelter belts, windbreaks and as isolated feature trees in paddocks.

ABOVE Local limestone feature walls imbue a strong sense of place while providing a textured backdrop to 1950s pots rescued from a roadside rubbish pile and collected shell treasures.

WILDLIFE – BIRDS, BEES AND OTHER IMPORTANT VISITORS

With our world's natural habitats diminishing at an astonishing rate, it is now critical to provide habitats for wildlife in our home environs, especially in urban areas, where ecosystems are highly fragmented.

Growing up, many of us provided birdfeeders full of seed, bottles of 'nectar' and threw stale bread onto the lawn to feed the birds. Today we know that the more responsible way to attract and support our native species is by providing safe and suitable habitat where wildlife can live and breed and by planting the right sort of food and shelter plants.

I consider wildlife-friendly inclusions in all my landscape designs today, depending on the client's brief and the location, condition and size of the site. A low-lying area on a site, prone to inundation, may be ideal for a wetland or bog. Another drier site may have space for an expanse of native grasses, ideal habitat for small seed-eating birds and insects. Other sites are so small that possibly there is only space for a nesting box, small pond, birdbath, an insect hotel and a few select plants for insects and birdlife.

Including plant species as a food source in our landscapes is one of the most important and effective methods of encouraging and supporting local wildlife. At Karkalla, watching the Eastern Spinebills and New Holland Honeyeaters visit correa flowers is an endless distraction we enjoy enormously. Old 1950s patterned concrete pots of *Kumara plicatilis* close to the living spaces provide much joy as we watch the birds dash in and out of the tubular orange flowers in winter. Other tempting plants to grow for nectar feeders are grevillea, salvia, cotyledon and echeveria. The selection of plant species does not need to be exclusively indigenous to your neighbourhood. Providing a diverse range of plants that flower at different times of the year, with multiple seed and nectar options, will support many species of wildlife.

On country properties, where space is not an issue, including or preserving indigenous plant species in a design to support specific animals or birds is to be encouraged. For example, she-oak *(Allocasuarina)*, a primary food source of the threatened Glossy Black-Cockatoo. Many native bird and mammal species also

LEFT Birdbaths and water bowls in the garden are magnets for wildlife. Shrubs and trees nearby provide fodder, protection and preening spots for birds.

need access to tree hollows for nesting, and retaining mature trees for their hollows is an important consideration as more and more bushland is cleared. Dead trees and fallen hollow branches make ideal homes for insects, birds and small reptiles and are interesting features in themselves.

Providing water for wildlife is necessary, indeed critical, during hot and dry times, when natural water sources may disappear, and water becomes scarce. While birds and insects can enjoy a pedestal birdbath, this is out of reach for an echidna, tortoise or small reptile. Ground-dwelling creatures require a lower source of water such as a pond or broad bowl placed at ground level. Water sources for wildlife can be many things – fixed and temporary – and ultimately the choice will depend upon your garden size, style and budget.

ABOVE The double flowers of *Papaver rhoeas* draw bees to the kitchen garden, increasing pollination in the surrounding plants and providing nectar for Karkalla's beehives.

RIGHT *Banksia integrifolia* provide nectar for a large variety of insects and birds and are a favourite for passing gangs of Yellow tailed Black Cockatoos.

SCALE

When I was a horticulture student, visiting gardens here in Australia and in Europe, it became apparent just how important scale is in a successful garden or plant composition. When something is perfectly scaled the eye can rest comfortably and elements look and feel balanced.

Scaling can be explained by sizing elements in a garden to relate carefully to what they are connected to. This is most probably a building or a view – borrowed or on site: the neighbours' trees, a cityscape, a body of water, hills, mountains or a town. The scale of the sky from different parts of the site requires consideration too.

In Australia, our skies are broad due to the continent's vast areas of open space, its relative lack of mountains and the predominance of low-rise cities. But everyone's access to sky is different: it can be a sliver; it can be massive.

If the sky is large and open or the adjacent building is large, the scale of the components in the garden needs to reflect this even if the available garden space is small or limited. Big views need generous gestures and broad strokes of plants.

Conversely, if the garden area is small and closely connected to the house, with little sky or open vista, the elements of this garden need to be nearer in scale to the interior elements. Here the garden takes the form of an exterior room and the size of the outdoor furniture, the colours and textures, may be selected to strongly connect the two spaces visually. This indoor and outdoor continuity will make the spaces feel larger as a whole, as in belonging together. As with small interior rooms it is better to err on the side of large outdoor elements rather than small as it tricks the eye into thinking the room is bigger than it is.

Human scale is what makes us feel at ease in a space. This is an important consideration for the areas you spend most time in outside. The addition of a pergola, a spreading tree canopy or a feature wall to give a sense of enclosure to a space can provide comfort.

When I first began designing country gardens, I came to appreciate very quickly that I needed to scale up. The useable spaces were generally larger, the skies and views broader, the houses larger or sprawling rather than two storey – the size of the garden elements needed

LEFT *Tetrapanax papyrifer* and *Banskia integrifolia* draw the eye up, balancing the height of the façade and the chimney. Small shrubs alone would fail to balance the scale of the house.

ABOVE A mass of plant textures emerge from this protected slope and combine with a single olive tree to balance the height of the stone walls and scale of the sea.

to reflect this increase or they would appear poorly chosen and inadequate. This does not mean the garden itself has to be large but the scale of elements in it still need to connect to the broader scene through paying attention to proportion, mass and void. I learnt the solutions are relational: generous seas of the one plant species needed to be larger, tree species bigger, pergolas more substantial, openings wider.

Designing landscapes in the country initially put my sense of scale to the test. We soon adopted techniques we still use today to ensure we can comfortably scale elements, often pegging out the design as we go. With walkie-talkies (although now we use smart phones), stakes, tape, and plenty of walking, we can determine tree positions, gate and fence locations, spots for garden beds, the position and height of a structure and other landscape features. Then and now it is about constantly refining a layout until we feel we have it right.

Pegging out a site is a useful visual tool. Once pegged out it is possible to walk around the garden and house viewing the proposed element from all angles. This can be done with some or all the elements until the garden is set out in its entirety. It gives form to a sketch but is entirely temporary and adjustable: it's just a more structured version of shaping a garden bed than using a garden hose. I revisit the site a few days later if possible and freshly observe the layout and adjust if necessary.

Taking photographs is also helpful in scaling, as larger elements, like a pergola, can be drawn onto photographs taken from different vantage points and the size, style and orientation experimented with.

Getting the scale right with vegetation comes with challenges of its own, remembering that scale also relates to time. It can be difficult to have and hold a long-term vision when it comes to plants. Newly planted vegetation begins small – often from tiny plant cells, tube stock and only sometimes more advanced specimens – and takes time to grow. It can therefore take years for the perfect scale to be reached and the vision achieved. It can be useful to overplant in these situations to gain more 'bulk' quickly, with some vegetative components being removed further along. There is always the risk though that the thinning doesn't occur – for example, if the property changes hands or notes are lost – and the garden remains overcrowded, with what were supposed to be temporary place-holders.

GARDEN DESIGN

ABOVE *Koelreuteria paniculata*, in lush full leaf, combined with stands of *Allocasuarina littoralis* behind the building provide an intermediary layer of vegetation that links the garden proper with the towering eucalypts behind.

NEXT PAGE A well-designed pergola is a human-scaled element that provides a strong link between house and garden. Large-leaved *Vitis coignetiae* provides welcome shade when needed and turns deep red in autumn.

MASS, VOID AND TEXTURE

One of garden design's principles is the considered use of mass and void. The most pleasing garden compositions and arrangements, the ones that truly catch the eye, have a structure built on mass and void, and delivered through texture and contrast.

In a garden, plants are generally the mass. This can be made up of single specimens of species combined with groups, drifts or substantial ribbons and bands of other species. The mass is best displayed next to a void – a surface or area which is usually of a single material and is a calming, unfussy space to rest the eyes. A void also shows off the plant textures of the mass to best advantage. The void can be a finely textured sea of granitic gravel, a rendered wall, an area of green lawn, a large hedge or still water in the form of a water bowl, lake or ocean. It's up to each gardener or designer to decide the void to mass ratio they want in their garden.

For me, texture is everything. And it plays a leading role in mass and void. Texture is vital in creating the contrasts within the mass. This ultimately determines the nature and personality of any design whether it be architecture, painting or landscape. Voids are not texture-less but about subtlety of texture. A lawn has texture, but it is not prominently textured – nor is a tactile, rendered wall. Textures are both seen and felt: the peeling bark of a *Betula utilis* var. *jacquemontii*; leaves that brush against you, or you yearn to touch; crunchy gravel or the cool of a stone path underfoot; the pattern of an aged brick wall; or the feel of silky-smooth sand beneath bare feet.

ABOVE Strategically manipulated *Allocasuarina verticillata* and *Alyxia buxifolia* provide rounded masses of texture balanced by voids of gravel, water tank and sky.

ABOVE Plant texture is your friend in a small garden. With careful pruning plenty of light can shine through *Lagerstroemia indica* x *fauriei* 'Tuscarora', underplanted with *Pittosporum tobira* 'Miss Muffet', a lush *Hydrangea quercifolia* and *Dianella tasmanica,* with Victorian Pyrenees Quarries slate as the foreground void.

Textures are also important to design because they are imbued with meaning and memory associations. In garden design, visual texture is more important solely because we see all elements in a garden, but we don't necessarily touch them all. The play of textures against each other and layering of different surfaces manipulates the mood or atmosphere in the garden context. Simple, smaller, repetitious textures can be calming and restful. Louder, larger textures can evoke excitement and exhilaration. Textures can draw the eye up or down or through, make spaces appear larger or smaller, induce peacefulness or stir up a party.

The layering of textures in a garden context is how a designer gives a scene depth and interest and ultimately creates a mood. The seasonal play of light and shadows on a stone wall, the considered placement of foliage textures in front of and behind a wall, the way the paving material is laid on the nearby path, the addition of ornaments or features all determine the atmosphere and style of the landscape as a space.

LEFT & RIGHT Voids can be created from a single species such as mass planted *Poa poiformis* var. *ramifer*, lawn, seas of granitic gravel or a simple wall.

Plants are the dynamic and living mass of our gardens and can add so much more than simply greenery. A particular plant's appearance is made up of the foliage texture and colour, that of its trunk and bark, any seed heads, its silhouette, as well as its form and habit. And then there are its flowers. How a plant is placed in the landscape, how it is treated and what other plants it is placed next to determine the planting style and mood. The mood may be varied as you move through the various landscape spaces, depending upon their use, by altering type, arrangement and treatment of the species. For example, homogenous drifts of fine textured and softly coloured tussocks that move in the breeze create a very relaxed mood. Conversely, closely clipped, dark coloured shrub species will create a heavier atmosphere; the landscape will be strongly anchored but less playful. The use of both of these species and treatments in juxtaposition may create a scene that is anchored by the clipped balls of shrubs but has movement in the waving tussocks in between.

When it comes to weighing up the balance of any landscape design, it can be useful to try and analyse the scene by imagining it in black and white, without the distractions of colour. Stripping off the colour can help you see the arrangement of mass and void and consider the interplay of textures as they actually are.

FOCAL POINTS AND FEATURES

Focal points and features in a landscape context can be many things – moveable or fixed, man-made or natural. Sculpture, an oversized and ornate pot, a gnarled tree, an architectural plant, a wisteria-covered arbour, an attractive outbuilding, a reflective pond or fountain could all be used to give a garden a focus. It is important to provide an element for the eye to rest on. A focal point is a well-placed and proportioned feature to draw the eye in, deliberately standing out from the background. Whatever the feature for focus, it is important to leave space around this element for it to breathe and be noticed.

Features can also be used to entice people through a garden and give a space meaning or sense of place. Providing glimpses of garden features – a stone outcrop, a rustic bench or sea view – creates intrigue and encourages exploration in the same way that paths curving out of view do. Some landscape features may already exist on a site, such as built elements or established vegetation, and the garden can be designed with this in mind, with a complementary feature added to highlight the original if necessary.

When introducing a focal point, consider the character or style of the garden, its location and size, your tastes or those of a client, and budget of course. Assess how any potential focal point will sit in the landscape: scale relative to space, proportion and harmony. A small sculpture in an expansive setting will go unnoticed, and similarly a substantial piece in a small space can be overwhelming. I like to develop ideas about a feature's origin, style and scale from the outset, so garden planning can evolve with the idea in mind.

ABOVE With its interior thinned to show off its sculptural boughs, *Melaleuca armillaris* makes a wonderful feature tree in any garden.

SCULPTURE

A much-loved focal point at Karkalla is the piece 'Koonya Beach Columns' by New Zealand sculptor Chris Booth. Built in situ in 1997, this sculpture of five tall stone totem poles is constructed from limestone and sandstone. It was designed for a particular location in the garden, so its scale and materials were carefully considered. It feels like it is of that place and helps reinforce the character of the site and its location. The home-made 'Thong Tree' is similar in this sense as it is made from hundreds of washed-up thongs we collected during a camping trip and beach clean in Arnhem Land. It cost little to build except time and effort in bringing them back to Victoria. It's a bit of fun and it links summer's emblematic footwear to the beach and Karkalla's oceanside location. We also have carefully positioned a Tiwi Island Pukamani pole on the front terrace as a landscape feature. Its ochre colours and timber complement the foliage textures and colours arranged there.

In the bushland areas we've strategically positioned other sculptures, to draw people through the coastal scrub. A galvanised steel sculpture by Melbourne-based metal sculptor Jonathan Leahey draws visitors to the gate to the national park and celebrates an anniversary for David and me. A glimpse of part of a tall sculpture, like the tops of 'Koonya Beach Columns', for example, is intriguing. Garden visitors love to explore and discover these surprises in the garden, and they imbue different areas with interest and connection to the broader location.

When I'm recommending a sculptor to a client, I like them to meet so they can work to develop some ideas together. A model or maquette of a sculpture can be made and photoshopped into a photograph of the garden space, to assist the designer and client to visualise the element in place. Alternatively, a more affordable approach may be to fashion something of your own. Second-hand shops, garage sales and roadside rubbish collection are usually rich sources of adaptable odds and ends – old coppers that can be used as pots, baths or tubs as ponds or parts of machinery as solid pieces of infrastructure or interest. Making your own feature or focal element is good fun, enormously satisfying and adds personal meaning to your garden.

LEFT This reclaimed pier post has impeccable credentials as a sculpture in an informal coastal setting. A young specimen of the weeping *Agonis flexuosa* 'Burgundy' perfectly offsets its strong sculptural form.

ABOVE The copper birdbath is the focal point in a narrow garden area that draws the eye through to it's reflective surface.

RIGHT The giant *Agave americana* provides a striking focal point that highlights the front door entrance. At night the up-lit agave creates additional drama.

PAGE BEFORE The view to the bay is framed by olive trees that have been carefully manipulated. Oversized clams and large 1950s concrete pots decorate a gravel terrace. Balls of *Correa alba* and *Alyxia buxifolia* mimic distant treetops.

ABOVE A fitting vintage decoration for a lakeside setting. The light shining on the garden beyond the house draws you in and through.

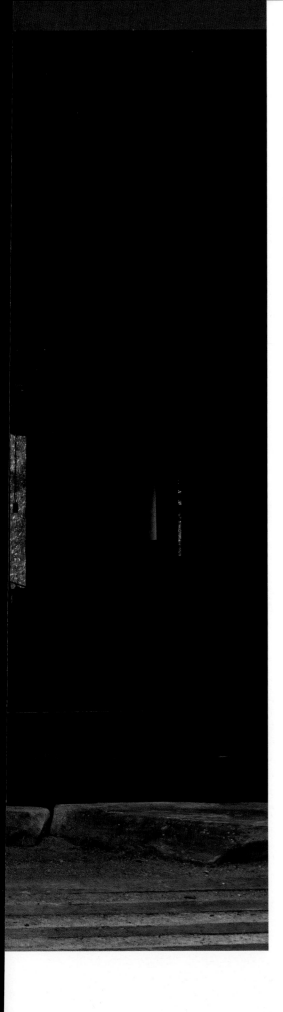

Use local materials to develop garden features and useable areas, as you would to create successful interior and exterior connections. These materials represent the character of the broadest setting. Stone, timber and textured concrete are attractive and reliable options. At Karkalla we have used local limestone in the house and garden walls, recycled aged pier timbers in retaining walls and as benches and posts, and old channel markers as focal points. Other found marine objects such as whalebones, sea-worn glass, driftwood, old fish traps or cray pots could also be used, sparingly, to reinforce a seaside garden sense of place. But don't overdo any of these features or decorative elements; use restraint and give each piece due consideration as to its inclusion and placement.

Borrowed landscapes and views can also be the focal point or feature of a landscape space. Good views are usually obvious from the outset, but a borrowed landscape can only be borrowed if it can be seen. Sometimes better views are made when they are framed but borrowed views may first have to be revealed by the removal of an obscuring element like a hedge or fence.

Clients are often reluctant to block or interrupt any part of a view, especially ones they have paid handsomely for. This is understandable – until you can show them that many views become more special by framing them. If you can see all of a view all of the time you tend to take it for granted. However, restricting a view from one area and then opening it as a surprise from another can triple the effect.

ABOVE 'Man Woman' by Melbourne-based metal sculptor Jonathan Leahey overlooks the rear gate and provides a strong focal point in the Karkalla garden.

RIGHT Carved stone pillars of Harcourt granite, which act as steps in the concrete tank pool, provide a sculptural element to the interior, especially when viewed from above.

Conversely, views or borrowed features might be obscured from the outset – maybe unnoticed by a new owner – and require unveiling. There is nothing more exciting than revealing a mountain vista, a sea view or that of a beautiful church spire or a neighbour's handsome tree when an existing element on a site is removed or carefully pruned. Recently we removed a large mass of weedy vegetation from the boundary of a Portsea garden to reveal a stunning view of a lake that is lit with gold at sunset.

When we first built Karkalla we planted about eight olive trees, around and on the front terrace, near to the house. At that time, we lacked privacy and protection from the prevailing winds and felt very exposed. Twelve years later those metre-high babies had become chunky giants despite the limited water, hydrophobic soil and tough conditions. It was time to reassess these view blockers. Some were removed and others were pruned up to accentuate their sensuous smooth trunks and frame the important views. This is the ongoing balancing act: streetlights and neighbouring houses to screen versus views to frame and admire. We also constantly weigh up the much-needed protection the olive trees offer from the ocean winds that can fill the top-floor gutters with sand blown from Koonya Beach 300 metres away. Nonetheless, once a year we use the pole saw to open up and sculpt the olives to advantage, as we do the *Allocasuarina*.

Designers may plant more trees or shrubs than are ultimately required, to provide clients with privacy, shade and shelter quickly. This can be at the short-term expense of a view or vista. Acacia trees are a good example of a species that may be used as a colonising or space-filling tree. They grow quickly, are short lived and can be removed when other more desirable species catch up. It is important that next steps for this temporary arrangement are communicated to and remembered by those that own or maintain the garden landscape or they may risk losing the view beyond the screen.

COLOUR

Colour determines the mood, the atmosphere, your experience of everything – consciously or not. A jumble of brighter colours excites the senses and a 'sea of one colour', especially a cool colour, can be restful and soothing or even possibly boring.

I was aware of the power of colour from a young age thanks to our mum's love of colour and design: in architecture, interiors and gardens. Colour was considered throughout our home and the colours and textures of our living room furniture were repeated in the garden it was connected to. Floor-to-ceiling windows enabled this visual connection and flow from inside to outside. Bright peacock-blue in silk cushions was reflected in drifts of blue Dutch irises and domes of echiums. The yellow of textured scatter cushions was repeated in the sunny spires of aeonium flowers, yellow Dutch irises and variegated flaxes and box balls. Our sofa and armchairs were covered in the same muted green of much of the foliage outside. We also had flowers for picking and arranging in the house: Mum favoured branches of magnolia and crab apple, bowls of violets and daphne and the spiced scent of wintersweet and honeysuckle.

I know from experience that when clients say 'I want lots of colour in my garden' they are referring to flower colour not foliage. Edna Walling understood: 'As if green isn't a colour,' she commented ruefully. I concentrate on the selection and arrangement of plants based on plant habit, foliage colour and texture rather than just flower colour. The foliage is what you observe for four seasons of the year (unless deciduous), whereas most flowers are fleeting, present for only short bursts of glory. I regard flowers generally as a bonus rather than a raison d'être.

RIGHT Burnt reds of *Hylotelephium spectabile* 'Autumn joy' are repeated around the patio, with purple shows from echium, verbena, rosemary and lavender. Plant arrangements based on flower colour often work best if tonally similar.

LEFT 'As if green is not a colour,' Edna Walling liked to say. Nuanced changes in foliage colour provide an interest that is subtle and calming, particularly welcome when you are aiming to create a restful space. *Berberis julianae* 'Spring Glory' is one of those plants whose foliage gently changes from coppery tipped to dark green with the season.

My approach to garden design is summed up in this maxim: foliage before flower. The range of greens is almost infinite when developing a planting design. Depending on the atmosphere you are aiming to create in a landscape space I select the palette of foliage greens as one would select any range of colours. Consider greens that complement, contrast, excite or calm. Acid green, grass green, brownish green, burgundy-green, reddish green, olive green, pale grey-green, blondish green, Eucalyptus green, bottle green: the adjectives are many, as are the plants to draw from. Flower colour, if conspicuous, requires consideration simultaneously. It is not an easy task when overall plant suitability is also of paramount importance – ultimately one does have to assess multiple plant attributes and the multi-taskers tend to rate well.

To build a plant palette for a garden space I produce lists of foliage-driven plants in categories – trees, large shrubs, medium shrubs, small shrubs, tussocks, ground covers and climbers – which I know will grow easily in that space and lend a desired look. Then I go through the lists to see if any of the plants produce flowers that will be conflicting with the overall scheme; I might remove, reduce, or relocate that plant. Once a comprehensive but manageable list has been created, I go about figuratively painting in the primary foliage colour or arranging the landscape space with these colours (plants), keeping in mind habit, texture and leaf colour. It is important to keep in mind that smaller spaces can generally handle much less variation in plant species than larger spaces without creating a riot. I do not necessarily use all the plants on the list, but the 'paint' is at hand on the palette if required. It's rather like collecting too many colour swatches from a paint shop: it's good to see how combinations work together and you can keep the allied or second-best colours on file.

ABOVE *Austostipa stipoides* combined with *Helichrysum microphyllum* and rosemary makes for some strong foliage variation, despite them all possessing fine foliage.

When designing planting schemes, I like to think of Gertrude Jekyll, the British horticulturalist, garden designer and artist who took up garden designing when her failing eyesight meant that painting was no longer easy for her. It didn't matter that she could no longer clearly see details in a garden – she looked at mass and void, especially at the texture and colour of both, as she arranged a garden space. A century later I also favour these impressionistic sweeps in gardens, although I do tend to favour the texture, colour and habit provided by foliage in comparison to Jekyll's fondness for flowers.

Although my approach to landscape design and planting schemes generally considers foliage and plant habit before obvious flower colour I do not want to be classed as anti-flowers. I love flowers – particularly observing the phenomenal process of flowering. In our Karkalla kitchen garden, I grow many bright and flamboyant flowers for picking and as fodder for birds, bees and other plant pollinators. Dahlias, sunflowers, a variety of poppies, sweetly scented sweet peas, drifts of lavender, snapdragons, ginger lilies, nasturtium and hollyhocks are my favourites and form a smorgasbord of colour. The sunflowers are a source of delight to the seed-eating birds, and a freshly picked bunch on the kitchen bench is a joy to behold. I also love the burst of vivid yellow fluff in early winter that the *Acacia podalyriifolia* produces, then the heralding of spring with the bright blue spires of echium.

ABOVE Deciduous trees like *Lagerstroemia indica x fauriei* 'Tuscarora' are bright with new growth in spring, with loud flowers to brighten the dappled shade in the height of summer. It's in autumn that we see them at their warm-toned peak where they complement the colour of the sculpture by Joanna Hodes.

LIGHT IN THE LANDSCAPE

If garden design is essentially about the creation of various harmonious spaces in an outdoor realm, then the role of natural and artificial light plays a big part in showing the way and guiding us through the garden spaces. Natural light is, of course, fundamental to the growth of healthy, robust and shapely plants, and their requirements when it comes to light should guide their placement. In the design realm, however, the important role of natural light is a little more esoteric. I firmly believe it is essential to understand and appreciate natural light and how it influences the mood in a garden space. Its functional cousin, artificial lighting, is both practical and can add a sense of drama to a garden. Altering lighting can be an expensive afterthought, so far better to contemplate both forms thoughtfully at the outset.

The influence of natural light in a garden changes through the seasons and throughout the day and can be used to great effect. One of the reasons I love phormium, cordyline and the large-leaved aeonium is the way sunlight 'bounces off' their leaves, particularly in the mornings and evenings and during winter when the sun is taking a lower path in the sky. This reflection illuminates the garden, giving brightness and joy to an otherwise potentially dull scene. Light also shines through the leaves of some large-foliaged plants in

a striking way, bringing an element of magic to a garden space. Small-foliaged plants tend to fully absorb sunlight and become supporting characters on the garden stage. From this, you can see how the mood of a garden can be manipulated to advantage. Large-foliaged plants can look wild and exotic, so use them to create drama. Use smaller-foliaged plants to lend calmness to a scene – unless pruned into crazy shapes, of course.

Light requirements for particular zones and purposes should be considered at concept stage. If a shady space is required for sitting out of the sun and dining or relaxing, then larger spreading trees can be utilised, or a vine-clad pergola installed. A kitchen garden needs an open sunny area for successful food production and shade-producing elements should be kept to a minimum. Similarly, lawn areas perform better without large trees casting excessive shade and competing for available water. That said, the amount of light that gets through large shrubs or trees can often be enhanced through judicious species selection, careful spacing and regular canopy or interior thinning.

Light can also be artificially introduced into garden spaces for night-time use and enjoyment. This is important as a functional aspect – to enhance safety when it comes to navigating steps and paths – but also to create a particular mood. At night it can be reassuring to see into garden spaces adjacent to those zones used at night, by having additional lighting beyond the entertaining area. Lighting can extend the boundaries of rooms and create interest beyond the house proper. Peering into a black space is neither interesting nor comforting.

ABOVE The subtle back-lighting of a scene can create intrigue and a special atmosphere. Light bounces off the large broad leaves of *Phormium tenax*, *Banksia integrifolia* and the trunks of *Melaleuca armillaris* in the background.

Strategic lighting of favourite garden features or plants can be used to dramatic effect or to draw the eye through a garden at night by creating and lighting a focal point. For example, the uplighting of *Tetrapanax papyrifer* creates a bright ceiling since the huge leaves are pale underneath and the shadows they create will dance on any nearby façade, creating theatre not experienced by day. This could be used to illuminate the way to a gate or front door simultaneously, achieving safety and interest together. Uplighting a pergola's posts and illuminating the foliage of overhead climbers has a similar effect and creates beautiful soft lighting under which to dine at night. Lighting a coloured feature wall in the garden at night can visually connect an internal space strongly with this external space and extend its boundary. Similarly, the lighting of a water feature can create a spectacular scene in the night-time garden.

The type and position of garden lights needs to be carefully thought through once the concept plan is complete. I recommend buying good quality lights for most outdoor purposes. We don't use solar light fittings, as to date we have found them to be inferior for the situation; they have a shorter life cycle and require the solar receiver to be in adequate sunlight to sufficiently charge the light to suit its purpose in the design. This is not practical for many applications such as uplighting a tree, where the fitting is positioned under the shade of the canopy; or next to a path where safety lighting requires reliable luminosity, including on overcast or winter days with less solar radiation. We would normally recommend that a home's solar system, where installed, is designed with sufficient capacity to accommodate the power requirements for running garden lights.

I like to err on the side of 'less is more' when it comes to artificial garden lighting. An over-lit garden can be startling rather than restful and interesting. Similarly, poorly positioned lights may shine directly in people's eyes and be more dangerous than helpful. Additional lights, if required, can be added at a later stage; however, if a garden is over lit from the beginning it is unlikely that lights will be removed.

All this mood and security lighting is lovely for the resident but do consider the impact of your outdoor lighting on neighbours and wildlife: be sensitive to the light's reach and brightness; set up timers or be sure to turn them off when you no longer need them. Light pollution is increasingly problematic for city dwellers and nocturnal animals.

ABOVE Decorative Japanesque lighting casts a low beam over *Themeda triandra* 'True Blue' and *Lomandra labill* 'Evergreen Baby'. A well-placed path light at knee height illuminates the organic rock step leading to the front door.

ABOVE Shadows cast by the sun or artificial light can be used to great effect to add texture and atmosphere. Here the shadows across the front door are created by the balustrade above and *Ginkgo biloba*.

121

ARRANGEMENT

The elements of a garden are arrived at by seeking a brief from the client. The placement of various elements in a garden and the appearance of these elements – their size, shape and organisation – is what informs the concept design; put simply, what goes where and what it looks like. Each feature or element is a part of the whole, and the organisation within the garden space and how the elements balance each other are critical. By comparison it is similar to the composition of a painting – except a garden is a dynamic scene, since every time we move around a garden space the composition changes with our whereabouts. And, additionally, gardens grow with time. That is a challenge in garden and architectural design and any three-dimensional design field.

Consideration of what you see and how it changes when you move through the various spaces of a garden or building or around a sculpture adds complexity to these design fields. When creating a concept design, I think through and plan the functional placement of landscape elements, but I also visualise how these elements will be viewed from different positions in the garden and from inside the house, to create a pleasing picture. I look at the concept from different angles, often in black and white, to see if I have got the balance and contrast right and that it conveys the desired mood.

Some zones of a garden need to be more functional than others. The useability and enjoyment of those semi-utilitarian spaces can be maximised through clever and considered layout of the elements. Finding solutions to those practical considerations can lead to energy and cost-saving advantages too.

Group elements which require regular access together, to improve efficiency and ease of movement. For example, having the kitchen garden and compost bins together, near the clothes line, perhaps on the way to a chicken coop and run, makes an efficient loop for daily

LEFT This planted arrangement looks just as good from indoors as outdoors and provides a strong link between the two, with dark green carpet evoking the forest floor. *Lagerstroemia indica x fauriei* 'Tuscarora' branches that have been thinned over time are silhouetted next to *Euphorbia wulfenii*, *Pittosporum tobira* 'Miss Muffet', *Mahonia aquifolium* and climbing *Parthenocissus quinquefolia*.

access. While hanging out the washing you can let the chickens into their run, feed them food scraps, check the vegetable garden and see how the apricot tree is faring. Often these elements have similar irrigation, feeding and shelter requirements. Practical groupings such as these are time saving and improve the functionality of the garden. Even in smaller gardens this is an important consideration, so a herb garden might be best placed near the clothes line.

At Karkalla, planting a kitchen garden and orchard adjacent to the house would have been desirable but the strong winds and lack of topsoil in that position made it impossible. We took advantage of the deeper soil and wind protection offered by a hollow north of the house. Vegetables, herbs, orchard trees and chickens are grouped and thrive in this sheltered, warm microclimate.

First thing in the morning, chickens are released into their run and fed, compost is emptied into the bin, the kitchen garden checked, and bits and pieces may be harvested for the day's meals. Hardy herbs are cultivated nearer to the kitchen, beneath the classic Hills Hoist. The washing line is positioned to take advantage of the energies of wind and sunshine and is close to the laundry.

When I'm happy with the concept design and it has been drafted I present it to the client. This plan includes the addition of various photos to assist in the visualisation of ideas. This early response outlines the various materials and elements, as well as planting ideas only. The detail, certainly of actual plant species I intend to use, comes later once the concept is resolved. Working in these stages – from the basics of mass, void, scale and the textures of materials to the eventual decoration of

ABOVE Understanding how a client will use spaces and move through the garden informs the conceptual layout of elements (photograph Will Salter).

ABOVE A simple timber bench is built into the retaining wall to provide a place to rest while gardening. This area within the walled kitchen garden is a combination of orchard, edible woody herbs, flowers for picking and others for the pollinators. All these plants have similar requirements so the arrangement of them together in the one space adjacent to the house is logical.

the planted areas, with suitable textures and colours – you develop a layered story with which to satisfy a brief.

Sometimes the arrangement of elements needs to be tweaked on site. This may be once vegetation is cleared or pruned, the house is built or the landscape construction underway and the new garden layout experienced in situ. It is usually a response to time or growth. Vegetation grows larger with time and may also change shape. Some plants also lose their leaves, and this may open views, reduce the overhead canopy and create a lighter brighter space. Either sort of change causes an alteration in scale and potentially people's experience of the space; some adjustment in response is usually desirable to maintain the design.

ABOVE The arrangement of these garden spaces according to use is both functional and beautiful. Outdoor dining combined with a fireplace and relaxed seating is positioned on a deck to the north of the house. Beyond, dispersed plantings of trees and underplanting provide shade, interest and habitat. The well-tended and curved lawn draws us through the garden.

CONSTRUCTION

Being involved in the construction or implementation phase of a landscape design leads to the best possible outcome for the client and the designer. This hands-on approach ensures a particular level of finish and allows for potential modification or adjustment of the design during the construction phase if necessary. Through regular visits on site the designer can see if an aspect of the design does not appear quite right, and it allows for correction. If it is not possible to visit the site, troubleshooting can still take place via photographs sent by the contractor or client. It is a good idea to encourage regular communication with the contractor for this reason and often an issue can be resolved this way and a site visit avoided.

For the past twenty-seven years I have been fortunate to work with David Swann, my partner in life and work. An engineer by vocation, David is a landscape contractor with a perfectionist's approach. David and his skilled team constructs as many of the gardens I design as he physically can. He possesses a fine eye for proportion and is particular about detail and finish, essential in crafting beautiful landscapes which are built for longevity. Working together for so long, we've developed something of a professional shorthand between us. It requires far less explanation and documentation of landscape elements than is common between contractor and designer and is built on a high level of trust. This is a large cost saving for clients, and we gladly explain the benefits of our association, usually while we show them examples of successful past projects.

ABOVE Once the house renovation and extension were complete, construction of the garden spaces began. Initially the large linking off-form concrete walls were built, followed by the long-raised garden beds. Paving was next, then the timber battened fences, irrigation, soil improvement, gravelling, planting and finally mulching.

ABOVE Appealing organic texture of a smooth, crazy-paved slate path. The laying of crazy paving is akin to tackling a large jigsaw puzzle.

RIGHT The construction of a curving pool fence requires a fine eye and careful attention to detail to get the curve just right.

During the construction phase I like to make regular site visits to ensure that the design feels right and to check construction detail. Anomalies beneath the ground are often found with the first turning of the soil. Bedrock and other obstructions such as a disused water tank may dictate a modification or reconfiguration in the design. If the house is also in the process of construction, internal views into the garden spaces can be analysed. It may be that a features and level survey is not entirely accurate or something on site changes during the house building phase. Issues can be rectified if identified early: a step may need to be added or subtracted from a flight of steps, a landing increased in size, or an undesirable feature in a neighbouring property hidden by additional vegetation. Since permits are not required in most instances for many elements of a landscape construction, the design is ready for small changes.

At times during the construction phase clients may decide to add an element to their garden; over the years we have added kitchen gardens, car parking spaces, in-ground trampolines, basketball rings, fire pit areas and vine-covered pergolas. Good designs have some flexibility built into them for this very reason.

Variables that may not have been apparent on earlier site assessments can become obvious during the implementation stage. Soil peculiarities, sun and shading patterns, the effect of wind from different directions and its strength (especially after existing buildings or vegetation has been removed), and traffic noise may impact the design and warrant a small adjustment. The additional information learned from these later visits allows you to finesse a planting design that is carefully considered and site appropriate. It is always beneficial to allow this design component to occur as late as is practicable in the construction process. This allows you to physically walk through the house and garden with the client to hone ideas and confirm plant choices. In my experience, most clients connect deeply with the project at this stage.

MAINTENANCE

'A garden is only as good as the maintenance it receives.' I was at university when I first heard this wise and unattributed mantra, and I learnt over the subsequent thirty years designing gardens that it is true.

Gardens require the correct care to realise a designer's intent. Ultimately, the success of any garden is not only appropriate plant choices which thrive but a tailored care and maintenance program. A skilled designer knows how to effectively communicate these requirements to those caring for a garden – and into the long term, including if the property changes hands. In addition to preparing a maintenance schedule, it is important to ensure the carer of the garden has a thorough understanding of each plant's requirements going forward too.

This does not apply so much to the general care of plants, but more to the clipping and shaping of shrubs and trees to achieve a particular look or size. If two olive trees are planted to frame a view and are never pruned, they may soon block out much of what you had intended to be framed. The intent was, over time, that olive branches would be thinned, the canopies pruned up and the silvery gnarled trunks emphasised, not obscured by dense foliage. How often do we see rows of overgrown plants encroaching over a path or driveway when the intent was to neatly hedge?

All plants, except annuals, grow larger with time, unless they are strictly pruned to a particular shape or size. This growth can be controlled, or the plants can be left alone to obtain their natural shape and size. Most gardens are a mixture of both control and abandon, as well as periods when there are gangly shapes and awkward gaps. Not all the plants in a garden scheme will be at the desired shape or size or bulk at the same time, just as all the plants which need pruning will not do so at once. Thus, a garden design is never perfectly realised because gardens are always growing and changing. It helps to view a developing garden as a work in progress, continually evolving to reveal unexpected delights.

ABOVE Olive branches are pruned up every two or so years and mounds of *Alyxia buxifolia* and *Correa alba* clipped perhaps twice a year, depending on the season. The more plants are watered the more they grow and the more clipping they require.

ABOVE *Cordyline species* emerge from a neatly clipped hedge of *Murraya paniculata*. High trimming like this may be best left to a professional, as part of a regular maintenance routine.

PRUNING AND SHAPING

In Australia during the 1970s, people began to experiment with bush gardening, planting native species, with little to no maintenance pruning or follow -up. The thinking of the time was that no interference was best, and as a result many species outgrew their locations, caused damage or died. Many plants gained a reputation for looking scruffy and the movement itself fell out of favour. What was almost certainly required for most of the plants was a good regular haircut, to increase new growth and control their size and shape.

When I was starting out, I thought valuing and using native plants was a missed opportunity, and it troubled me that so many Australian species were not considered as worthy garden inclusions by the majority of garden owners and designers. Since that time, of course, we have become more knowledgeable about the diversity of species, but also how to care for them.

Pruning of plants increases their longevity through a process of continual rejuvenation, which is a bonus when considering a garden's lifespan and the cost of replacing plants. When I began pruning many of the local species I planted at Karkalla, I had not seen it done before in a horticultural context. I was experimenting with how hard to prune, when to prune and in what style.

Designers approach the manipulation of plants in a variety of ways depending on the look and atmosphere they are intending to achieve. It is advisable to have a good understanding of how different species respond when pruned as not all plant groups can survive hard pruning. As my confidence grew, so did the variety of species I inflicted my shears upon.

I have been interested in plant manipulation since I first observed how the elements of wind, snow and salt affect naturally occurring plant communities. I like the way plants in nature are sheared into sometimes bizarre or at least intriguing shapes. *Eucalyptus pauciflora*, twisted *Melaleuca lanceolata*, *Leucopogon parviflorus* that crawl along rocky ledges and bonsaied white correa specimens all caught my attention at times. As gardeners we can emulate the effects of nature with a pair of secateurs or hedge shears.

Clipping some plants definitely makes them more garden worthy. *Alyxia buxifolia* is a good example of this. In the wild, it is often an ungainly shrub, and it can grow haphazardly in sheltered positions. In our garden, we prune it into large solid shapes that show off its handsome leathery dark-green foliage and brilliant green new growth. It is the only species indigenous to the south of the Mornington Peninsula that has this leaf type. Pruned to advantage, generally twice a year, it helps to visually anchor a planting scheme of species with paler smaller leaves.

At Karkalla I have had the space and confidence to experiment over the years. The approach I've adopted is regular pruning of shrubs and trees nearer to the house, and less interference as you move away from the house. It's a simple and useful design tool and it demonstrates how you can marry a garden with its broader, more natural or wild setting.

ABOVE This row of *Myrtus communis* was established to create privacy for the upstairs bedrooms. As they established, lower foliage was removed to show off their beautiful trunks and create space below for other plants. In this way a second level of interest could be established.

CARE AND MAINTENANCE

It is helpful to divide maintenance into two areas. This is dependent upon frequency: regular tasks which may happen weekly, monthly, quarterly or yearly like lawn mowing, checking irrigation heads in summer, plant feeding of various areas, sowing broad bean seeds, raking leaves, cleaning of paved areas. Then there are specialist or irregular tasks like tree canopy thinning or crown reduction, lifting and dividing of bulbs, cleaning out the water tank, repotting of potted plants, taking cuttings of a shrub or staining a fence. These tasks may only need carrying out on an irregular basis; however, it is important that you remember when they are carried out. The activities can be organised by zone in a larger garden or by plant type or season.

How the tasks are organised or delegated is a practical consideration, dependent on the size and style of the garden, its location and the amount of time and involvement the garden owner wishes to contribute. It may be possible to allocate the tasks to two maintenance groups or two people, based on their skills. Regardless of who looks after a garden, it is important to develop a care and maintenance program that is not only available in written form but is thoroughly understood once a garden has been planted. I like to walk over the site with the carers to make sure they are familiar with the various tasks, to identify potentially problematic areas and other concerns. An irrigation system and its programming for different times of the year needs to be worked through, and digital and laminated copies of the planting plan supplied. This way if a plant dies or is damaged, the correct species can be identified and bought in replacement. With a care and maintenance program in place, it remains important to make regular site visits during the first year to keep a close eye on plant growth and help solve problems that may arise.

It's just as important for home gardeners, regardless of the garden's size or type, to keep track of care and maintenance activities. This can be organised into a diarised month-by-month program outlining what activities are to be done when. For example, March – feed all kitchen garden beds. Repeat in October. Alternatively, keep a notebook or soft copy files listing tasks on an activity basis. For example, training all deciduous climbers after leaf drop in autumn. This way activities can be marked off when completed and one-off garden events can be recorded too: beetroot seeds sown 14 July, *Eucalyptus gregsoniana* from Speciality Trees planted 30 October. I highly recommend this level of documenting. I often assume that I am going to remember a lot of this information but seldom do, especially when it comes to plant origins and dates of sowing or planting. Later on, if a problem occurs with a plant or you would like to purchase another of the same genotype it is possible to trace its origins.

Depending on a garden's location, I will recommend care and maintenance people I've worked with before, if possible, and remain in close communication with them. Often a quick conversation or a photograph can identify and solve a problem very quickly and efficiently. With all of this in place, I believe it is important to visit our gardens at least a few times a year to assess their successes and possible failures and chat with the owners to make sure they are happy with the direction the garden is growing in. Remaining involved with the garden development and its owners provides the opportunity to adjust the garden over time. We greatly value the relationships we have developed with many clients over thirty years of designing, implementing and caring for landscapes.

As a garden designer, nothing gives more joy and fulfilment than happy clients. Seeing people enjoying their outside spaces, jumping on trampolines, children playing in cubby houses, harvesting food from their kitchen gardens, lying in the shade of a tree, picking flowers, and generally interacting with the natural world makes my role as a designer feel immensely satisfying and valuable.

LEFT Broad beans are well supported in a steel and bamboo frame. The inspiration for this came from a photograph my clients took in Italy. Repair jobs to plant supports are best made during the non-growing months.

ABOVE Backyard and patio citrus will benefit from regular feeding, watering and careful pruning but will reward you well. Grabbing a homegrown lemon for a recipe is ridiculously satisfying.

ABOVE Sometimes maintenance looks simple enough, however, if the garden designer's intent is not understood things can go awry. This garden scene requires very little maintenance to keep it looking like this and heavy-handed clipping or hard cutting back of these tussocks is undesirable. *Poa labillardieri* and *Lomandra longifolia* 'Tanika' as understorey and *Eucalyptus macrandra* and *Koelreuteria paniculate* as canopy plants.

ABOVE *Agonis flexuosa* 'Burgundy', *Westringia fruticosa* and *Phormium tenax* 'Anna Red'
thrive under the existing canopies of *Melaleuca armillaris*. Plants should be able to develop
with time, to make their own pictures.

WITH TIME

With time plants grow and gardens change. Trees particularly need tending to over the years, to direct growth and manage their ultimate structure. This formative pruning is a sensible approach so major structural flaws like bifurcation can be avoided. This is the development of two leaders from one main trunk, which with time creates a structural weakness and a potentially dangerous situation. Crown thinning may also be required to allow more light to reach the understorey planting. If this is carried out regularly and by someone who approaches it with knowledge and creativity it will be barely noticed. Engage an arborist to oversee tasks involving trees as they mature.

It is important to understand that there does come a time in a tree's development that can cause conditions beneath the canopy to alter to such a degree that the understorey plants need reassessment. Ground covers that initially enjoyed a sunny open situation may need replacing with shade-loving species that survive in a drier, shaded niche created by trees' growth. It is not always possible to select plant species that will thrive in both those conditions – hot sun and dry shade – and fulfil the role you need them to. It is, however, important to design a garden where understorey plants do not require replacement in their entirety. Landscape designers and architects have an important responsibility to understand what different plants require to thrive and to confront change.

While I was at university I developed a restoration management plan for an old Edna Walling garden in inner Melbourne. As part of it, I compared what Walling planted in the 1920s to the growing conditions over sixty years later. Instead of recommending the replanting of Walling's original scheme, I developed categories of Walling favourites by plant needs, through analysing old photographs and reading widely. From this I designed new planting schemes suited to the altered conditions, both climatic and situational. This way the garden could be restored sympathetically as an Edna Walling garden, using the plants she favoured but planting designs tailored to the times.

Gardens may change hands and, when possible, I like to remain involved with the garden's evolution. New custodians may have different requirements or tastes, and by remaining involved you can assist the new carers to become familiar with the garden and guide any changes. I encourage a year at least for any new owner to experience the 'new' garden before embarking on changes.

The fact that plants grow and gardens evolve and change with time is perhaps the biggest challenge and joy of gardening. There is never an exact moment where a garden can be called complete or finished; it is more about the journey of enjoying its continual growth and now-ness. This is made up of fleeting garden moments: plant groupings which take your breath away, harvested food enjoyed by friends and family, a bench in dappled tree shade, a sanctuary from the outside world. The rewards of gardens are many, and they will continue to change and delight.

ABOVE *Betula utilis* var. *jacquemontii*, *Ginkgo biloba* and *Miscanthus transmorrisonensis* all enjoy similar conditions and have matured together to create a scene which changes with the seasons.

RIGHT Karkalla is a beloved work in progress. Many plants self-sow in these seas of gravel and keeping or moving many of these additions means parts of the garden are continually changing. This type of adaptability is the key to its ongoing success.

THE
GARDENS

146

ABOVE Clockwise from front: *Cotyledon orbiculata, Alyxia buxifolia, Aeonium arborescens* and *Dianella revoluta var. brevicaulis* all enjoy the same conditions and combine to make a vibrant composition of interesting foliage textures.

SIGNATURE PLANT LIST

TREES

Acacia podalyriifolia	Mount Morgan wattle
Agonis flexuosa 'Burgundy'	burgundy willow myrtle
Allocasuarina littoralis	black she-oak
Allocasuarina verticillata	drooping she-oak
Banksia integrifolia	coast banksia
Betula utilis var. *jacquemontii*	Himalayan birch
Brugmansia suaveolens	angel's trumpet
Cercis canadensis 'Forest Pansy'	eastern redbud
Citrus x limon	lemon
Eucalyptus leucoxylon 'Rosea'	pink-flowered yellow gum
Jacaranda mimosifolia	jacaranda
Lagerstroemia indica x fauriei 'Natchez'	crepe myrtle
Laurus nobilis 'Miles Choice'	bay
Leptospermum laevigatum	coastal tea-tree
Leucopogon parviflorus	coast beard-heath
Melaleuca lanceolata	moonah
Olea europaea	olive
Pyrus nivalis	snow pear

SHRUBS, SUBSHRUBS

Alyxia buxifolia	sea box
Banksia praemorsa	cut-leaf banksia
Berberis julianae 'Spring Glory'	wintergreen barberry
Callistemon 'Kings Park Special'	bottlebrush
Cordyline stricta	slender palm lily
Correa 'Marian's Marvel'	native fuchsia
Correa alba	white correa
Correa reflexa var. *nummulariifolia*	roundleaf correa
Cotinus coggygria 'Grace'	smokebush
Cotoneaster horizontalis	rock cotoneaster
Daphne odora	winter daphne
Euphorbia characias subsp. *wulfenii*	wulfen's spurge
Grevillea lanigera 'Mount Tamboritha'	woolly grevillea
Grevillea olivacea	olive grevillea
Hydrangea quercifolia	oak-leaf hydrangea
Leucadendron 'Safari Sunset'	
Mahonia aquifolium	holly-leaved barberry
Nandina domestica	sacred bamboo
Phlomis fruticosa	Jerusalem sage
Pittosporum tobira 'Miss Muffet'	
Rosmarinus officinalis var. *prostratus*	prostrate rosemary
Tetrapanax papyrifer	rice-paper plant
Westringia fruticosa	coastal rosemary

BAMBOO

Bambusa textilis var. *gracilis*	slender weavers bamboo

PERENNIALS, SUCCULENTS, GROUND COVERS

Aeonium undulatum	stalked aeonium
Ajuga reptans 'Jungle Beauty'	bugleweed
Alocasia macrorrhiza	elephant ears
Canna x *generalis* 'Tropicanna'	canna lily
Hedychium gardnerianum	Kahili ginger lily
Hylotelephium telephium 'Matrona' (syn. *Sedum*)	stonecrop
Kumara plicatilis (syn. *Aloe*)	fan aloe
Lamium galeobdolon	aluminium plant
Pelargonium tomentosum	peppermint geranium
Plectranthus ambiguus 'Nico'	
Plectranthus ciliatus	
Pratia pedunculata	trailing pratia
Senecio mandraliscae	blue chalksticks
Verbena bonariensis	Argentinian vervain

TUSSOCKS, STRAPPIES

Anigozanthos 'Big Red'; 'Orange Cross'; 'Yellow Gem'	kangaroo paw
Arthropodium cirratum 'Matapouri Bay'	New Zealand rock lily
Austrostipa stipoides	prickly spear-grass
Dianella revoluta var. *brevicaulis*	coast flax lily
Dietes bicolor	yellow wild iris
Dietes iridioides 'White Tiger'	false iris
Lomandra labill 'Evergreen Baby'	
Lomandra longifolia 'Tanika'	spiny-head mat-rush
Miscanthus transmorrisonensis	evergreen miscanthus
Phormium tenax 'Anna Red'; 'Surfer Boy'	New Zealand flax
Poa labillardierei 'Eskdale'	common tussock grass
Poa poiformis var. *ramifer*	dune poa
Themeda triandra 'True Blue'	kangaroo grass

CLIMBERS

Parthenocissus tricuspidata 'Lowii'	Boston ivy
Vitis coignetiae	crimson glory vine

ABOVE *Banksia integrifolia* provides height while anchoring this garden scene of *Phormium tenax*, *Helichrysum microphyllum* and *Austrostipa stipoides*.

MEDITERRANEAN CLIFFTOP

PORTSEA

OWNERS	
Mandy and Edward	
LOCATION	
Southern end Mornington Peninsula	
SITE DESCRIPTION	
Clifftop, sloping, open	
ARCHITECT & DATE	
Bell Fisher Architects, new house, 2014/2015	
PROPERTY SIZE	
1675 m²	
GARDEN DESIGNED & IMPLEMENTED	
2015	

Tucked into a cliff shelf, overlooking Port Phillip, this site is all about the view. The house consists of two stone-clad pavilions connected by a glass spine, set low and comfortably recessed in the landscape, and the cliff falls away to the beach below. The house faces north, and the design incorporates both the stunning bay view and a couple of heroic old moonah trees.

Entrance to the property is from the southern edge of the block, which slopes down from the front gate to the house; access to the front door is via a series of substantial cypress pine steps of varying width combined with gently exposed aggregate. The steep slope is densely planted with a mosaic of Mediterranean species including olives as specimen trees, *Euphorbia* x *martinii* 'Ascot Rainbow', *Cistus* x *laxus* 'Snow white', *Echium candicans*, *Convolvulus mauritanicus* and *Phlomis purpurea* 'Alba', combined with native species, some locally indigenous. Repeated for mass, form and texture are *Austrostipa stipoides*, *Viola hederacea*, *Correa alba* and *C. reflexa* var. *nummariifolia*. It's a feast of grey-blues, greens and smudges of gold – there is much for the eye to explore.

The east-facing inner courtyard is pre-dominantly enjoyed as a kitchen garden and sheltered sitting and dining area. It is planted with citrus trees towards the boundary, a hedge of *Laurus nobilis*, *Dietes bicolor* and favourites such as English lavender, rosemary and other herbs. Raised beds produce an abundance of vegetables for the house and flowers abound for bees and other insects.

Continuing from the courtyard, a simply planted slate path passes an outdoor shower towards the bay. Here a long deck wraps itself across the front elevation and around an ancient sculptured *Melaleuca lanceolata*, which provides shade and scale and frames the view perfectly. A plunge pool with a horizon edge sits on this level also and echoes the colour of the bay. A small, curved area of buffalo and *Dichondra repens* lawn is incorporated below the deck and surrounded by indigenous plantings repeated naturally in the landscape beyond. The boundary area was stabilised with retaining elements, weed matted and revegetated. In turn this has softened the view of the structure from the beach below.

A small courtyard on the western side of the axis houses another *Melaleuca lanceolata*. The tree is a spectacular feature by day and at night when it is lit up. *Cordyline stricta*, *Viola hederacea* and *Dietes bicolor* act as supporting characters.

This is a landscape which is imbued with a sense of belonging, through seas of textured plants, a carefully chosen palette of materials and a design which accommodates and honours the surrounds.

LEFT Olives on this embankment are maintained to a particular height to provide a connection with the scale of the house. Lifting their canopies allows the mix of Mediterranean-style planting to drift across the slope and move with the wind.

PLANT LIST

TREES

Citrus x latifolia	Tahitian lime
Citrus x limon 'Eureka'	lemon
Jacaranda mimosifolia	jacaranda
Laurus nobilis 'Miles Choice'	bay
Leucopogon parviflorus	bearded heath
Olea europaea	olive
Prunus armeniaca 'Moorpark'	apricot

SHRUBS, SUBSHRUBS

Abutilon x hybridum 'White cv.'	Chinese lantern
Cistus x laxus 'Snow White'	
Correa alba	white correa
Correa reflexa	native fuchsia
Correa reflexa var. nummulariifolia	roundleaf correa
Echium candicans	pride of Madeira
Euphorbia x martinii 'Ascot Rainbow'	Martin's spurge
Grevillea olivacea	olive grevillea
Lavandula angustifolia	English lavender
Phlomis 'Edward Bowles'	Jerusalem sage
Phlomis purpurea 'Alba'	white Jerusalem sage
Rosmarinus officinalis 'Blue Lagoon'	rosemary
Westringia fruticosa	coastal rosemary

PERENNIALS, SUCCULENTS, GROUND COVERS

Agave attenuata	swan's neck agave
Convolvulus mauritanicus	
Crassula ovata	jade plant
Crinum pedunculatum	swamp lily
Dichondra repens	kidney grass
Viola hederacea	native violet

TUSSOCKS, STRAPPIES

Austrostipa stipoides	prickly spear-grass
Cordyline stricta	slender palm lily
Dianella revoluta var. brevicaulis	coast flax lily
Dietes bicolor	yellow wild iris
Dietes iridioides 'White Tiger'	False Iris
Lepidosperma gladiatum	coast sword-sedge
Phormium tenax	New Zealand flax

CLIMBERS

Passiflora edulis	passionfruit

ABOVE Plants were chosen to reflect the earthy hues in the feature stone walls and steel canopy and to provide year-round interest. Spent flower heads such as the *Echium candicans* are left in the name of beauty.

153

THE GARDENS

ABOVE View across the driveway towards the front entrance steps of silvered cypress pine, where shadows from the pruned olive create organic patterns.

LEFT The rusted colour of this sculpture, 'Whirling Figure' by Greg Johns, echoes that of the front door canopy with its shape picking up the flowers of nearby *Echium candicans* and *Phlomis purpurea* 'Alba'.

MIDDLE Early morning dew drops on the arching leaves of *Austrostipa stipoides,* with mounds of *Euphorbia* x *martinii* 'Ascot Rainbow' and *Correa* drifting in the background.

RIGHT *Crassula ovata, Euphorbia* x *martinii* 'Ascot Rainbow', *Dianella revoluta*
var. *brevicaulis, Echium candicans* and *Leucopogon parviflorus* surround
Cistus x *laxus* 'Snow White', in a tapestry of textures.

157

ABOVE The view across the plunge pool to the bay, where new indigenous plantings on the cliff create texture and a natural softness.

MEDITERRANEAN CLIFFTOP

ABOVE The view under the ancient *Melaleuca lanceolata* through the glass-covered walkway between the house pavilions. Beyond is the east facing courtyard which contains the kitchen garden and space for outdoor dining.

ABOVE The kitchen garden is sited in a sheltered courtyard and elevated to provide an easily accessible area in which to plant tend and harvest.

BELOW The long timber deck wraps itself around a *Melaleuca lanceolata*, and steps float down to an organic-shaped lawn, flanked by indigenous plantings.

162

ABOVE In the west courtyard, late afternoon light filters through another old moonah onto *Cordyline stricta*, *Correa reflexa* var. *nummulariifolia* and *Viola hederacea* below which thrive in its abundant shade. The clothes line and service area sits behind the timber screen (centre).

ABOVE Blooms of *Dietes iridioides* 'White Tiger' brighten the early morning shadows and flank the long lawn.

ABOVE Large flags of slate near the outdoor shower are interplanted with *Dichondra repens*, which loves the extra water. Balls of *Westringia fruticosa* and clumps of *Dianella revoluta var. brevicaulis* soften the side battened fence, with an apricot tree overhead.

165

BAYSIDE JAPANESE

BEAUMARIS

OWNERS	
Keith and Phyllis	
LOCATION	
Suburban bayside Melbourne	
SITE DESCRIPTION	
Medium-size, flat, open	
ARCHITECT & DATE	
Zenibaker Architects, new house, 2017	
PROPERTY SIZE	
925 m²	
GARDEN DESIGNED & IMPLEMENTED	
2017/2018	

Wrapped around a newly built Modernist-style house in Melbourne's bayside suburbs, this garden celebrates a Japanese aesthetic. The owners had a big hand in the layout and finishes throughout the house and were equally keen to be involved in many of the exterior material and plant choices.

The low-slung house was designed without a front fence, in keeping with other examples of the style. The role of the open front garden is to draw visitors towards the house and maximise the connection with the streetscape. For privacy and security, a brick wall and gate exist closer to the house and its front door.

A mature jacaranda, carefully retained in the build, is the beautifully sculptured anchor point for the front garden. It and a large *Tristaniopsis laurina* in front of the property provide much-needed canopy in summer for this exposed area. A heavy layer of clay subsoil dictated many of the new plant choices.

The garden has a modern Japanese feel through the restrained arrangement of plants and materials, more than the plants themselves. The design of the front path drew inspiration from a photo supplied by the owner and is made up of organically shaped slabs of sawn Victorian bluestone, surrounded by grey pebbles. Adjacent to the driveway, offcuts of bluestone were also used, on edge, to emulate a riverbed.

The owners requested Australian plant species to provide food and habitat for local birdlife and many of the plant choices celebrate this. See-through tufts of *Themeda triandra* 'True Blue', *Lomandra longifolia* 'Tanika', *Correa* 'Tucker Time Dinner Bells', *Correa reflex* var. *nummulariifolia*, *Banksia spinulosa* 'Birthday Candles' and screens of *Westringia fruticosa* combined with *Callistemon viminalis* 'Slim' were used to create a textural feast in the front. An *Agonis flexuosa* 'Burgundy' is a graceful feature tree, *Phormium tenax* 'Anna Red' provides form and *Cercis canadensis* 'Forest Pansy' frames the entry. This elegant smooth-barked tree is repeated at the threshold to the house and creates a spectacular autumn show.

The remaining garden spaces link strongly to the interior and are viewed through tall and wide windows that wrap around the rear of the house. Mossy aged landscape rocks and slabs of bluestone are used in the garden to add organic texture and an unfussy functionality.

Greening and blurring of the boundary fences was achieved with tall, narrow growing *Acmena smithii* 'Green Screen', *Nandina domestica* and *Parthenocissus tricuspidata* 'Lowii'. Feature shrubs include more callistemon, bird-attracting *Banksia ericifolia* and *Phormium tenax* 'Surfer Boy'. *Ginkgo biloba* is the focal tree of the patio. Repeated tussocks used at the rear and sides include *Lomandra labill* 'Evergreen Baby', *Ophiopogon japonicus* around the bluestone stepping stones, and the large *Dietes robinsoniana*, from Lord Howe Island, with its swords of white flowers. The owners have added elements such as a Japanese stone water bowl and Frank Lloyd Wright–inspired garden lights, as a personal touch and as fitting additions to a house and garden that successfully combine to form a whole.

LEFT Sawn bluestone pavers embedded on their edge give the impression of a creek bed alongside the driveway and are softened by *Phormium tenax* 'Anna Red' and other tussocks.

PLANT LIST

TREES

Acer palmatum 'Seiryu'	Japanese maple
Acmena smithii 'Green Screen'	lilly pilly
Agonis flexuosa 'Burgundy'	burgundy willow myrtle
Cercis canadensis 'Forest Pansy'	eastern redbud
Corymbia ficifolia 'Calypso'	flowering gum
Ginkgo biloba	maidenhair tree
Hakea laurina	pin-cushion hakea

SHRUBS, SUBSHRUBS

Allocasuarina glauca 'Cousin It'	she-oak
Banksia ericifolia	heath-leaved banksia
Banksia spinulosa 'Birthday Candles'	dwarf hairpin-banksia
Callistemon viminalis 'Dawson River Weeper'; 'Slim'	bottlebrush
Correa 'Tucker Time Dinner Bells'	native fuchsia
Correa reflexa var. *nummulariifolia*	roundleaf correa
Leucadendron 'Safari Sunset'	
Nandina domestica	sacred bamboo
Persoonia pinifolia	geebung
Philotheca myoporoides	long-leaf wax flower
Westringia fruticosa	coastal rosemary

PERENNIALS, SUCCULENTS, GROUND COVERS

Myoporum parvifolium 'Purpurea'	boobialla
Pratia pedunculata	trailing pratia

TUSSOCKS, STRAPPIES

Anigozanthos flavidus	kangaroo paw
Dietes robinsoniana	Lord Howe wedding lily
Lomandra labill 'Evergreen Baby'	
Lomandra longifolia 'Tanika'	spiny-head mat-rush
Ophiopogon japonicus	mondo grass
Patersonia occidentalis	long purple flag
Phormium tenax 'Anna Red' 'Surfer Boy'	New Zealand flax
Themeda triandra 'True Blue'	kangaroo grass

CLIMBERS

Trachelospermum jasminoides	star jasmine

ABOVE Early morning light catches the foliage of *Banksia ericifolia* and the feature rocks, and a curved masonry wall in the background holds the scene and provides additional seating. A single *Ginkgo biloba*, underplanted with *Lomandra labill* 'Evergreen Baby', grows from a circle in the gently exposed aggregate.

ABOVE The wide modern facade of the house is punctuated with seas of tussocks and the larger feature plants *Phormium tenax* 'Anna Red' and *Cercis canadensis* 'Forest Pansy'. A Japanese-inspired path leads visitors to the front gate and embedded landscape rocks anchor the space.

LEFT The textures of *Patersonia occidentalis*, *Ophiopogon japonicus*, *Banksia ericifolia* and *Correa reflexa* var. *nummulariifolia* merge around feature rocks, and a simple urn provides water for birds and insects.

MIDDLE *Cercis canadensis* 'Forest Pansy' arches over the front door, and in autumn its yellow leaves dance in the wind like a mobile. *Trachelospermum jasminoides* covers the wall behind and provides a sweet clove scent in spring.

RIGHT Sawn bluestone pavers from Victoria's Western District float in a sea of embedded pebbles. *Lomandra longifolia* 'Tanika' and *Themeda triandra* 'True Blue' soften the edges of the path with their arching foliage

ABOVE The east-facing bedroom window enjoys morning sunlight and a wide view of the side garden. *Philotheca myoporoides*, *Callistemon viminalis* 'Dawson River Weeper', *Leucadendron* 'Safari Sunset', *Patersonia occidentalis* and *Correa reflexa* var. *nummariifolia* attract birdlife into the scene.

LEFT *Gingko biloba* in its golden autumn glory catching the morning light. It's silhouetted against a neighbouring cypress to beautiful effect, with *Lomandra labill* 'Evergreen Baby' at its feet.

ABOVE The rear north-facing garden is higher than the internal living room floors and visually connects the two spaces. Landscape feature rocks are used to retain this rear area and provide access along the garden bed. *Banksia ericifolia* as a feature plant with *Anigozanthos flavidus*, *Lomandra labill* 'Evergreen Baby', *Correa reflexa* var. *nummulariifolia* and *Myoporum parvifolium* 'Purpurea'.

177

ORIENTAL SANCTUARY

TOORAK

OWNERS

Kathy and Nick

LOCATION

Inner suburban Melbourne

SITE DESCRIPTION

Sloping, shady, clayey

ARCHITECT & DATE

Kerstin Thompson Architects, new house, 2012

PROPERTY SIZE

750 m²

GARDEN DESIGNED & IMPLEMENTED

2012/2013

This inner-city site, after a new house build, presented multiple (and common) challenges: a clay base and poor drainage, overlooking issues from neighbours and a prominent house to screen on the downhill side. Its orientation offered a shady south-east facing rear garden and an exposed north-west facing front garden.

One of the biggest challenges in creating this garden – and needed to provide continuity – was to select species that were happy to thrive in all three areas. There are four or five versatile species that succeed across the zones and play a vital part in the overall design.

The solution for screening was to plant bamboo *Bambusa textilis* var. *gracilis* (a clumping variety), which has thrived in the heavier soil. This non-invasive species was planted on all three boundaries as soon as the house was finished, with earth shaping to give the screening a head start.

The street-facing front garden has no fence, but the boundary is defined by a hedge of *Murraya paniculata*. Height and shade are provided by a *Jacaranda mimosifolia* and *Lagerstroemia indica* that thrive in the heat. Behind this the planting is designed to create year-round interest with plants such as *Miscanthus transmorrisonensis*, *Garrya elliptica*, with its dangling catkins, *Camellia sasanqua* 'Plantation Pink', *Hydrangea quercifolia* and ground cover in the form of *Ajuga reptans* 'Jungle Beauty' and *Cotoneaster dammeri*.

Visitors are drawn through this planting into the entrance via a slate patio and to a gate of almost transparent mesh, which provides security without disruption of sight lines through the garden from front to rear. From there, visitors proceed to either the downstairs apartment or up a flight of stairs to the main home.

The courtyard is dominated by *Betula utilis* var. *jacquemontii*, their papery, peeling bark echoing the cream of the house brickwork. The very shady garden beneath is planted with lush green species, chosen for an Oriental feel, including *Fatsia japonica*, *Asplenium nidus*, *Hedychium gardnerianum*, *Clivia nobilis* and *C. miniata* (relocated from the owners' previous home) with *Lamium galeobdolon* and *Helleborus orientalis* as ground covers. Much of the rear garden is viewed from the terrace at the top of the stairs, and the planting was designed with this in mind.

Two tiers were designed in the rear garden. These level terraces were created using much of the slate and honeycomb rock from the original garden in the construction of the retaining walls and paths. The useable surfaces are topped with expanses of fine granitic gravel and provide a pleasant surface underfoot.

Betula utilis var. *jacquemontii* are repeated as feature trees against the bamboo and other layers of textured foliage, with seasonal highlights from *Berberis julianae* 'Spring Glory', *Hydrangea quercifolia*, *Abutilon* x *hybridum*, *Magnolia* 'Vulcan', *Miscanthus transmorrisonensis* and other shrubs. Ground interest is provided by the beautiful weeping mounds of *Liriope muscari* 'Emerald Cascade', *Anemone japonica*, more hellebores and tumbling *Cotoneaster dammeri*.

LEFT *Jacaranda mimosifolia* breaks up the long façade of this Modernist-style house and creates beautiful patterns of shadows. A *Murraya paniculata* hedge echoes the strong lines of the architecture and provides privacy for the garden spaces beyond.

PLANT LIST

TREES

Betula utilis var. *jacquemontii*	Himalayan birch
Citrus x *limon* 'Eureka'	lemon
Jacaranda mimosifolia	jacaranda
Lagerstroemia indica x *fauriei* 'Biloxi'	crepe myrtle
Magnolia grandiflora 'Kay Parris'	evergreen magnolia
Magnolia 'Vulcan'	saucer magnolia

SHRUBS, SUBSHRUBS

Rhododendron 'Kurume group'	Japanese azalea
Berberis julianae 'Spring Glory'	wintergreen barberry
Berberis thunbergii 'Silver Beauty'	Japanese barberry
Camellia sasanqua 'Plantation Pink'	sasanqua camellia
Chaenomeles speciosa 'Apple Blossom'; 'Nivalis'; 'Winter Cheer'	japonica
Chimonanthus praecox	wintersweet
Cotoneaster dammeri	bearberry cotoneaster
Daphne odora	winter daphne
Fatsia japonica	Japanese aralia
Garrya elliptica	silk tassel bush
Hydrangea quercifolia 'Pee Wee'	oak-leaf hydrangea
Mahonia fortunei	Chinese mahonia
Murraya paniculata	orange jessamine
Nandina domestica	sacred bamboo
Viburnum carlesii	Korean spice viburnum
Viburnum opulus 'Sterile'	snowball tree

PERENNIALS, SUCCULENTS, GROUND COVERS

Abutilon x *hybridum* orange cv.	Chinese lantern
Agave attenuata	swan's neck agave
Ajuga reptans 'Jungle Beauty'	bugleweed
Anemone x *hybridus* 'Deep Pink'	
Asplenium nidus	bird's nest fern
Bergenia cordifolia	heart-leaf bergenia
Dierama pulcherrimum 'Raven'	angel's fishing rod
Hedychium gardnerianum	Kahili ginger lily
Helleborus orientalis	lenten rose
Lamium galeobdolon	aluminium plant
Pratia pedunculata	trailing pratia

TUSSOCKS, STRAPPIES

Clivia miniata cream cv.; orange cv.; red cv.	kaffir lily
Miscanthus transmorrisonensis	evergreen miscanthus

CLIMBERS

Parthenocissus henryana	silver vein creeper
Wisteria sinensis	Chinese wisteria

ABOVE The internal courtyard with its entrance steps is filled with shade-loving plants including *Asplenium nidus, Hedychium gardnerianum, Helleborus orientalis* and *Lamium galeobdolon* providing a lush floor to this important space. The trunks of *Betula utilis* var. *jacquemontii* echo the colour of the off-white bricks and allow light to penetrate the house in winter.

182

ABOVE Looking through the fully planted courtyard space to the rear garden beyond. The wall-hanging was bought by the owners in Bali and is made from bottle tops.

ORIENTAL SANCTUARY

ABOVE The rear garden was designed to create a lush space when viewed from the second-floor living spaces. *Fatsia japonica*, *Wisteria sinensis* and *Agave attenuata* follow the edge of the slate path recycled from the original garden.

ABOVE *Berberis thunbergia* 'Silver Beauty', two-toned *Lamium galeobdolon*, strappy *Liriope muscari* 'Emerald Cascade' and *Hydrangea quercifolia* form a cool green pocket.

ABOVE The white blooms of *Hydrangea quercifolia* abut *Parthenocissus henryana* on the wall, with *Daphne odora, Garrya elliptica* and *Miscanthus transmorrisonensis* behind. The hedge protects them from the harsh sun.

RIGHT Slate steppers lead you to the garden beyond, through *Anemone japonica* and *Miscanthus transmorrisonensis,* with the broad leaves of *Fatsia japonica* overhead.

PAGE AFTER Honeycomb rocks and slate from the original garden are reused in the retaining walls and steps of the sunken garden. *Cotoneaster dammeri* falls over walls. From left: *Berberis julianae* 'Spring Glory', *Viburnum, Betula utilis* var. *jacquemontii, Agave attenuata, Fatsia japonica, Miscanthus transmorrisonensis* and *Anemone japonica.*

COASTAL
RETREAT

PORTSEA

OWNERS

Sam and Jim

LOCATION

Southern end Mornington Peninsula

SITE DESCRIPTION

Flat, large, open, low lying

ARCHITECT & DATE

Ray Dinh Architecture, new house, 2016

PROPERTY SIZE

3460 m²

GARDEN DESIGNED & IMPLEMENTED

2016/2017

Sweeps of tussocks and shrubs combine to reflect local coastal character in this casual family garden. It is designed for function and beauty, with generous decks and seating zones, a pool and in-ground trampoline. The level site is edged by neighbouring cypresses and some borrowed exotic trees, and it's a sheltered and private retreat.

The coastal site is low lying, protected from the sea winds, with a deep and reasonably rich sandy topsoil. The L-shaped timber and off-form concrete house is situated towards the rear of the block, leaving a large north-facing space at the front for most of the garden, a lawn for active play and parking for several vehicles. The large natural shaped plantings in this area soften the house, provide shade, year-round interest and encourage birdlife. There is also a small herb garden.

In response to the high water table, the finished height of the swimming pool was raised, but sits beautifully in its weathered timber deck, as if floating like a pontoon. Light reflects off the pale underside of *Banksia integrifolia*, where other grey and silver plants spill over and through the timber batten pool surround, with golden puffs of grasses, reminiscent of a dune.

Several existing tree specimens were retained, their twisted and multi-trunked bases tidied up to provide a sculptural element as well as dappled light through the mid-level. These included several *Lagunaria patersonia*, two *Melaleuca armillaris* and a *Leptospermum laevigatum* copse. Mixed underplantings rest below the raised canopies.

Gentle curves in the lawn, paths and sitting spaces blend into relaxed plantings of grasses and strappy plants adjoining the house. *Phormium tenax and P. tenax* 'Anna Red' are used, to provide bulk, mass and a touch of drama as much as colour. These are grouped with *Euphorbia characias* subsp. *wulfenii*, the bright flower heads like coral, and loosely shaped *Correa alba*, *C. reflexa* and *C. reflexa* var. *nummulariifolia* repeated in different beds near the house. Warm tones are seen in *Agonis flexuosa* 'Burgundy', a delicate small tree with downward hanging leaves and small blooms. *Tetrapanax papyrifer* was planted at the end of the outdoor dining area for interest and contrast next to the long expanse of dark exterior panelling.

Drives, paths and seating areas are well-proportioned and feature dun-coloured Dromana granite toppings and a neutral palette of slate crazy paving near the pool, complementing the paler timber façade at that end of the house. Reclaimed pier relics from Portsea add interest on arrival and are a solid historic link to the location.

LEFT A recycled pier pylon marks the arrival zone, underneath a *Melaleuca armillaris*, retained and pruned to enhance its sculptural form. *Tetrapanax papyrifer, Westringia fruticosa, Correa reflexa* var. *nummulariifolia, Dianella revoluta* var. *brevicaulis* and a flowering *Agonis flexuosa* 'Burgundy' spill to the gravel edge.

PLANT LIST

TREES

Agonis flexuosa 'Burgundy'	burgundy willow myrtle
Banksia integrifolia	coast banksia
Citrus x latifolia	Tahitian lime
Citrus x limon 'Eureka'	lemon
Leptospermum laevigatum	coastal tea-tree

SHRUBS, SUBSHRUBS

Alyxia buxifolia	sea box
Callistemon viminalis 'Slim'	bottlebrush
Correa alba	white correa
Correa reflexa	native fuchsia
Correa reflexa var. *nummulariifolia*	roundleaf correa
Echium candicans	pride of Madeira
Euphorbia characias subsp. *wulfenii*	wulfen spurge
Hydrangea macrophylla var. *normalis*	white lacecap hydrangea
Melianthus major	cape honey flower
Pomaderris paniculosa subsp. *paralia*	coast pomaderris
Rhagodia candolleana	seaberry saltbush
Rosmarinus officinalis 'Blue Lagoon'	rosemary
Tetrapanax papyrifer	rice-paper plant
Westringia fruticosa	coastal rosemary

PERENNIALS, SUCCULENTS, GROUND COVERS

Aeonium undulatum	stalked aeonium
Canna x generalis 'Tropicanna'	canna lily
Crassula multicava	fairy crassula
Hedychium gardnerianum	Kahili ginger lily
Helichrysum microphyllum	
Plectranthus ambiguus 'Nico'	
Plectranthus caninus	dogsbane
Pratia pedunculata	trailing pratia
Zantedeschia aethiopica 'Green Goddess'	arum lily

TUSSOCKS, STRAPPIES

Austrostipa stipoides	prickly spear-grass
Dianella revoluta var. *brevicaulis*	coast flax lily
Dianella tasmanica	Tasman flax lily
Phormium tenax	New Zealand flax
Phormium tenax 'Anna Red'	New Zealand flax
Poa poiformis var. *poiformis*	coast tussock grass
Poa poiformis var. *ramifer*	dune poa

CLIMBERS

Passiflora edulis	passionfruit

ABOVE *Poa poiformis* var. *ramifer* and *Dianella revoluta*
brevicaulis are planted along the gravel path behind
the pool creating a casual atmosphere.

193

ABOVE Outside the rumpus room is a semicircular patio of Pyrenees Quarries slate. *Banksia integrifolia* is repeated as a feature tree to attract bird and insect life, underplanted by *Helichrysum microphyllum* and *Austrostipa stipoides*.

ABOVE The inground trampoline is barely visible from the house within
a planting of *Agonis flexuosa* 'Burgundy', *Westringia fruticosa*, *Phormium tenax*
'Anna Red' and *P. tenax*. The pool fence snakes in the background behind
a retained *Melaleuca armillaris*.

COASTAL RETREAT

LEFT *Correa alba, Phormium tenax* 'Anna Red' and *Aeonium undulatum* combine to break up façade of house and give enclosure to the lounging area behind.

BELOW *Banksia integrifolia, Phormium tenax, Aeonium undulatum, Correa reflexa* var. *nummulariifolia* and *Agonis flexuosa* 'Burgundy' offer year-round foliage interest and fleeting flowers next to the void of lawn.

COASTAL RETREAT

LEFT We designed this spotted gum and copper rail pool fence to curve through the planting of flax and other soft plants.

MIDDLE Light plays on the trunks of *Melaleuca armillaris* and bright *Helichrysum microphyllum*.

RIGHT Mixed colours in the slate picks up many of those in the landscape as well as offering beautiful texture alongside *Helichrysum microphyllum, Austrostipa stipoides,* flax and *Banksia integrifolia.*

THE GARDENS

LEFT *Tetrapanax papyrifer* grows very quickly and creates interesting shadows in this outdoor shower space and entrance to the home.

ABOVE With time, tall-growing *Banksia integrifolia* will balance the height of the Monterey cypress on the garden's northern boundary.

URBAN FOREST

MALVERN

OWNERS

Creina and Michael

LOCATION

Inner suburban Melbourne

SITE DESCRIPTION

Flat, open

ARCHITECT & DATE

Spaces Pty Ltd, renovation, 2009

PROPERTY SIZE

1392 m²

GARDEN DESIGNED & IMPLEMENTED

2009

This urban garden renovation followed remodelling and an extension to the house. The owners were keen to keep as many of the existing mature trees on the site as practical, but other than that, the brief was clear: to create a lush, private garden that complemented their home.

The existing pool, new chunky pergolas and the retained specimen trees – an *Agonis flexuosa* 'Burgundy', a row of *Cupressus cashmeriana* and two *Phoenix canariensis* – partly informed the architectural structure of the new garden. The garden renovation concentrated on three aspects: the entrance, the pool and the planting design.

An inviting new pedestrian entrance was created, setting the tone for the rest of the garden. It is generously spaced and features irregular-shaped Pyrenees Quarries slate paving, a material repeated in other parts of the garden. Gentle paths with steps lead the visitor from the gate to the front door. The planting design in this area was to embed the existing trees and complement the simplicity of the entrance. *Dietes iridioides* 'White Tiger' are mass planted below the sentinel-like *Cupressus cashmeriana* to set off their grey, peeling bark, and a new planting scheme around a retained *Celtis australis* provides a simple, green frame to the garden beyond.

The second aspect of the remodelling focused on the pool area. The pool itself was modernised to relate to the more modern architecture of the extension. It was given cleaner lines by removing an internal spa, lined with new tiles and coping. The contemporary feel was enhanced by an eye-catching sculpture, a giant red rabbit by Joanna Rhodes, on a sea of pale gravel.

Throughout the garden, the role of the new planting design was to harmoniously incorporate the existing trees, link functional spaces, act as a screen and create a beautiful and useable garden space. A new lawn provides a solid green void to rest the eye as well as to cool the surrounds. Around the lawn is a marriage of exotic and native plants, layered in contrasting forms, colours and textures. *Cotinus coggygria* 'Grace' and *Canna* x *generalis* 'Tropicanna' set off the pale vertical trunk of the native *Angophora costata,* and *Hylotelephium spectabile* 'Autumn Joy' (syn. *Sedum*), *Lomandra longifolia* 'Tanika' and *Plectranthus ciliatus* provide interesting ground cover.

Dark foliaged plants are also used to give a greater sense of a rich green oasis, such as large sweeps of English ivy *Hedera helix* as a ground cover, *Philotheca myoporoides* and *Murraya paniculata* as structural shrubs and *Elaeocarpus reticulatus,* endemic to eastern Australia, to screen the neighbouring house. Fruit trees have also been included within the ornamental plantings of this cool and contemporary garden sanctuary.

LEFT Existing mature trees that include *Phoenix canariensis, Cupressus cashmeriana,* a massive *Agonis flexuosa* 'Burgundy' and *Celtis australis* form the framework for this urban retreat. Billowy seas of tussocks *Lomandra longifolia* 'Tanika' and *Dietes iridioides* 'White Tiger' create an understated understorey and lead the eye into a void of lawn.

PLANT LIST

TREES

Elaeocarpus reticulatus	blueberry ash
Ficus edulis	fig
Jacaranda mimosifolia	jacaranda
Lagerstroemia indica x fauriei 'Tuscarora'	crepe myrtle

SHRUBS, SUBSHRUBS

Cotinus coggygria 'Grace'	smokebush
Murraya paniculata	orange jessamine
Nandina domestica	sacred bamboo
Philotheca myoporoides	long-leaf wax flower
Rosmarinus officinalis 'Tuscan Blue'	rosemary
Sarcococca ruscifolia	Sweet Box
Viburnum suspensum	sandankwa viburnum

PERENNIALS, SUCCULENTS, GROUND COVERS

Agave attenuata	swan's neck agave
Canna x generalis 'Tropicanna'	canna lily
Crassula multicava	fairy crassula
Hedychium gardnerianum	Kahili ginger lily
Hylotelephium spectabile 'Autumn Joy' (syn. *Sedum*)	stonecrop
Pelargonium tomentosum	peppermint geranium
Plectranthus ambiguus 'Nico'	
Zantedeschia aethiopica 'Green Goddess'	arum lily

TUSSOCKS, STRAPPIES

Clivia nobilis	green-tip forest lily
Dietes iridioides 'White Tiger'	False Iris
Lomandra longifolia 'Tanika'	spiny-head mat-rush

CLIMBERS

Trachelospermum jasminoides	star jasmine

ABOVE The trunks of the Bhutan cypress frame the view to the lawn from the front entrance path. *Dietes iridioides* 'White Tiger' thrive in the dense shade beneath.

207

ABOVE Pyrenees Quarries slate is laid in local gravel as a transition zone from lawn to an area of solid crazy paving. Greyer tussocks of *Dietes iridioides* 'White Tiger' are repeated, as are *Lomandra longifolia* 'Tanika'. Autumn colour is from *Lagerstroemia indica* x *fauriei* 'Tuscarora'.

LEFT Sun comes through the retained *Agonis flexuosa* 'Burgundy' (rear) and *Celtis australis* (front), around the renovated original pool. This garden is all about the trees.

MIDDLE A corner with a rich tapestry of foliage. Flowering *Plectranthus ambiguus* 'Nico' is backed by multicoloured *Canna* x *generalis* 'Tropicanna' and *Zantedeschia aethiopica* 'Green Goddess'.

RIGHT Low *Murraya paniculata* hedges are used to divide the garden but are pruned to easily see over. Sculptured *Lagerstroemia indica* x *fauriei* 'Tuscarora' feature in a gravelled patio.

THE GARDENS

LEFT Crisp strips of lawn define the existing steps, underneath *Phoenix canariensis. Lomandra longifolia* 'Tanika' complements the palm's textured fronds. A stand of *Cupressus cashmeriana* that once defined a title boundary is inside the gate.

ABOVE Views of the lawn void through *Jacaranda mimosifolia* with *Cupressus cashmeriana* hanging above. The cupressus branches are regularly trimmed to achieve this.

ABOVE Crazy-slate paved small terraces or platforms lead from the gate to the front door and garden. *Celtis australis* has been pruned to show off the trunk and boughs and creates a carpet of yellow leaves. *Dietes iridioides* 'White Tiger' and the *Murraya paniculata* hedge soften lines linking to the poolhouse.

SEASIDE COTTAGE

PORTSEA

OWNER
Maggie
LOCATION
Southern end Mornington Peninsula
SITE DESCRIPTION
Sloping, small, divided
ARCHITECT & DATE
Richard Joubert Architects, house renovation, 2017
PROPERTY SIZE
920 m²
GARDEN DESIGNED & IMPLEMENTED
2017/2018

Down a steep driveway, hidden behind dense roadside bush, lies this single-storey weatherboard home on the coast. The owner purchased the property in 2015 and a renovation on house and garden began soon afterwards.

Gnarled *Melaleuca lanceolata* line the driveway, twisting and turning in the filtered light to beautiful effect. Potentially a difficult area to plant successfully, we had these protected trees dead-wooded and canopy thinned to show off their sculptural trunks and allow more sunlight to the understorey. This process in itself is rejuvenating. Here *Agave attenuata, Hydrangea quercifolia,* bicoloured *Zantedeschia aethiopica* 'Green Goddess', *Dietes grandiflora,* ground-hugging *Plectranthus ciliatus, Daphne odora* and violets providing foliage interest throughout the year and seasonal flower colour.

The two-tiered front garden space facing east was dark and dingy due to an enormous *Cinnamomum camphora.* Shade from the canopy extended over the house and mosquitoes reigned, making the area uninviting and unusable. Once the laurel was removed the useable space opened up significantly.

The owner's brief was simple. She imagined an outside lounging area near to the house, somewhere to enjoy a morning coffee with the paper or evening drink with friends. She described herself as a non-gardener, and this needed to be carefully considered when it came to plant selections.

Terracing was retained, using two walls of cypress pine. We extended the level area out from the house to balance its height and paved this surface with crazy Pyrenees Quarries slate to add an interesting texture. The colour palette in the slate ranges from pale to mid greys to a touch of chestnut and rust, and the variations provide a visual link to the colours seen in the garden.

A deep and long timber bench was built into the base of the lower retaining wall, and this was eventually dressed in large seat cushions covered in outdoor fabric for longevity. A higher timber bench for the barbecue to sit on was also installed to complete the brief.

Planting in this protected front zone includes many Mediterranean species. Clipped balls of grey-green *Teucrium fruticans* and domes of *Echium candicans* strongly anchor the planting while *Hylotelephium spectabile* 'Autumn Joy' (syn. *Sedum*), bursts of blue from *Ceratostigma plumbaginoides, Verbena bonariensis,* rosemary and *Iris germanica* provide year-round interest and fodder for birds and bees. A lemon and lime tree supply much-loved citrus and a herb garden thrives in the rich composted soil of the terraces.

Screening of the eastern neighbour and paling fence was achieved with a compact form of *Laurus nobilis* 'Miles Choice', clipped to create a green backdrop for the colourful planting.

A plunge pool was built in a sunny position on the western side of the block, and shade is provided by a wisteria-covered pergola. A productive vegetable garden was shared, up until recently, with a large tiger snake, since expertly caught and relocated safely into a national park.

LEFT Mediterranean-style planting complements the sloping site, which has been terraced with cypress pine retaining walls to create useable spaces. This front garden space includes *Agave attenuata, Hylotelephium spectabile* 'Autumn Joy', balls of *Teucrium fruticans,* lavender, rosemary, *Echium candicans , Verbena bonariensis,* other herbs for the kitchen and citrus in front of the shed.

PLANT LIST

TREES

Brugmansia suaveolens	angel's trumpet
Citrus x *latifolia*	Tahitian lime
Citrus x *limon* 'Eureka'	lemon
Laurus nobilis 'Miles Choice'	bay

SHRUBS, SUBSHRUBS

Correa reflexa var. *nummulariifolia*	roundleaf correa
Cotoneaster dammeri	bearberry cotoneaster
Daphne odora	winter daphne
Echium candicans	pride of Madeira
Hydrangea quercifolia	oak-leaf hydrangea
Lavandula angustifolia	English lavender
Nandina domestica	sacred bamboo
Rosmarinus officinalis 'Blue Lagoon'	rosemary
Teucrium fruticans	tree germander

PERENNIALS, SUCCULENTS, GROUND COVERS

Agave attenuata	swan's neck agave
Ajuga reptans 'Jungle Beauty'	bugleweed
Aloysia citrodora	lemon verbena
Ceratostigma plumbaginoides	blue plumbago
Plectranthus ambiguus 'Nico'	
Hylotelephium spectabile 'Autumn Joy' (syn. *Sedum*)	stonecrop
Thymus serpyllum album	white creeping thyme
Verbena bonariensis	Argentinian vervain
Viola odorata	sweet violet
Zantedeschia aethiopica 'Green Goddess'	arum lily

TUSSOCKS, STRAPPIES

Arthropodium cirratum 'Matapouri Bay'	New Zealand rock lily
Dietes grandiflora	fairy iris
Iris subg. *Nepalensis*	Himalayan iris
Phormium tenax	New Zealand flax

CLIMBERS

Jasminum azoricum	white Azorean jasmine
Passiflora edulis	passionfruit
Trachelospermum jasminoides	star jasmine

ABOVE Existing *Melaleuca lanceolata* on the driveway and around the entrance have been cleaned up and sculptured to show off their trunks and allow in more light. Underplanted by *Phormium tenax, Plectranthus ambiguus* 'Nico' and *Hydrangea quercifolia* for summer flowers and autumn foliage.

THE GARDENS

LEFT *Agave attenuata*, flowering *Plectranthus ambiguus* 'Nico', moonahs and *Phormium tenax* are part of a bold planting around the entrance. These species tolerate a variety of conditions and look good year round.

RIGHT *Hylotelephium spectabile* 'Autumn Joy' is used for long colour from summer to autumn and displays beautiful dead heads. Rosemary and balls of *Teucrium fruticans* are repeated in this area to anchor the garden scene, and a *Laurus nobilis* hedge greens the boundary and adds privacy.

THE GARDENS

LEFT Weathered cypress pine timbers complement the colours of the planting scheme. *Echium candicans* is centre of the upper tier; *Rosmarinus* 'Blue Lagoon' and common thyme spill over the lower terrace near a bowl of succulents.

ABOVE Overlooking the sheltered front nook, a well-used spot for morning coffee and evening drinks, and back towards the driveway and entrance.

LAKESIDE HAVEN

MAIN RIDGE

OWNERS

Amanda and Grant

LOCATION

Main Ridge, Mornington Peninsula

SITE DESCRIPTION

Sloping, open, lakeside

ARCHITECT & DATE

Meacham Nockles McQualter, new house, 2010

PROPERTY SIZE

12.7 ha (31.4 ac); 8130 m² garden area

GARDEN DESIGNED & IMPLEMENTED

2010/2011

Centre stage at this country house is the lake at the bottom of the hill, an ever-changing view, a welcome swimming spot and a haven for wildlife. The relaxed garden rolls down to the water's edge, successfully mimicking the planting of a natural lake margin or water course. Plant choices are mainly Australian native and complement the Scandinavian-style holiday home, which sits close to the earth, with an open and light aesthetic, a single step from the house into the outdoors.

The garden was designed in conjunction with the house, allowing for soil improvement after the house site was cut. Good onsite topsoil was combined with compost and manure to create a healthy planting medium, but much of the success of the garden was due to careful plant selection, including varieties which handle dry spells as well as periods of inundation.

Landscape materials were all local to Victoria and included Pyrenees slate for retaining walls and paving, local fine granitic gravel for the paths and recycled bridge timbers for steps and to define the entrance. A major feature in the garden are the clumps of *Anigozanthos* 'Big Red', which flower all summer into autumn and draw in honeyeaters and other nectar-feeding birds. *Vitis coignetiae* rambles over the pergola and provides welcome shade as well as brilliant autumn foliage.

Trees include the small gum *Eucalyptus macrandra*, with its stunning shiny trunks, she-oak *Allocasuarina littoralis* and the deciduous *Koelreuteria paniculata*. Mass planting of tussocks such as *Themeda triandra* 'True Blue' and *Lomandra longifolia* 'Tanika' and ground covers including *Grevillea lanigera* 'Mt Tamboritha', which flowers throughout winter, create soft swathes of vegetation that surround the house, connecting it strongly to the lake. The bold *Phormium tenax* 'Anna Red' have thrived in the wet conditions along with *Melaleuca nesophila* and the indigenous *Poa labillardierei*. As the garden has grown and more shade has been created by the developing tree canopies, especially on the east side of the house, some of the underplanting has been modified to include more shade-loving plants. The success of *Plectranthus ambiguus* 'Nico' and *Microsorum diversifolium* has allowed a continuum of low-lying vegetation.

The eastern side of the garden includes a cherished kitchen garden of vegetables, herbs and fruit trees and a chook house and run which are all tended by the family. The western side is dominated by a large treehouse that sits high up in a pine tree, complete with a flying fox that propels you toward the centre of the lake. This is a practical, productive and fun garden for all seasons.

LEFT For this soft setting for views to the lake, the void is made from local Dromana gravel, with plantings of *Poa labillardieri*, *Lomandra longifolia* 'Tanika' and *Anigozanthus* 'Big Red', and *Dichondra repens* forming a tight ground cover

PLANT LIST

TREES

Allocasuarina littoralis	black she-oak
Citrus x latifolia	Tahitian lime
Citrus x limon 'Eureka'	lemon
Citrus x paradisi	grapefruit
Cydonia oblonga	quince
Diospyros kaki	persimmon
Eucalyptus macrandra	long-flowered marlock
Ficus edulis	fig
Koelreuteria paniculata	golden rain tree
Melaleuca nesophila	honey myrtle
Morus nigra	black mulberry
Prunus armeniaca 'Moorpark'	apricot
Prunus domestica 'D'Agen'	plum 'D'Agen'
Prunus salicina	blood plum
Punica granatum	pomegranate
Pyrus communis	pear
Pyrus pyrifolia	nashi

SHRUBS, SUBSHRUBS

Banksia spinulosa 'Birthday Candles'	dwarf hairpin-banksia
Callistemon viminalis 'Hannah Ray'	bottlebrush
Correa baeuerlenii	chef's hat correa
Correa pulchella var. *minor*	native fuchsia
Correa reflexa var. *nummulariifolia*	roundleaf correa
Grevillea lanigera 'Mount Tamboritha'	woolly grevillea

PERENNIALS, SUCCULENTS, GROUND COVERS

Microsorum diversifolium	kangaroo foot fern
Plectranthus ambiguus 'Nico'	
Viola hederacea	native violet

TUSSOCKS, STRAPPIES

Anigozanthos 'Big Red'	kangaroo paw
Dianella tasmanica	Tasman flax lily
Lomandra longifolia 'Tanika'	spiny-head mat-rush
Poa labillardierei	common tussock grass
Themeda triandra 'True Blue'	kangaroo grass

CLIMBERS

Vitis coignetiae	crimson glory vine

ABOVE *Melaleuca nesophila,* with its papery twisted trunks, grows out of *Lomandra longifolia* 'Tanika' with *Phormium tenax* 'Anna Red' on the right of the path – all plants that like boggy ground. Recycled jarrah give the parking area definition.

PAGE AFTER *Eucalyptus macrandra* and *Allocasuarina littoralis* are pruned to frame views to the lake from the terrace. *Correa baeuerlenii* in the foreground, like *Anigozanthos* 'Big Red', is included for summer colour and to attract birds.

ABOVE The pergola is an extension of the house, adding a shaded dining area, covered with *Vitis coignetiae*. Slate crazy paving from Pyrenees Quarries is an attractive textured surface underfoot. The use of standalone rock steps into the house is in the Japanese style.

ABOVE A semicircular space for lounging, overlooking the lake. The stacked slate wall retains the area, with *Correa reflexa* var. *nummulariifolia* falling over the stone, with *Poa labillardieri* (self-sown in gravel). *Eucalyptus macrandra* is repeated, with *Allocasuarina littoralis* for textural contrast. *Lomandra longifolia* 'Tanika' and *Banksia spinulosa* 'Birthday Candles' add interest and bird-attracting fodder to the upper level.

ABOVE Evening light dances on the water and illuminates tussocks, the strong inside-outside connection made via large glass sliding doors and floor-to-ceiling windows.

RIGHT *Allocasuarina littoralis* needles fall on this rear garden path and beds like a gentle blanket. *Plectranthus ambiguus* 'Nico' was added as shade increased, as was the fern *Microsorum diversifolium*.

LEFT *Alnus cordata*, a large drift of *Poa labillardiera* and an organically shaped stone bath create a private bathing nook overlooking the lake.

MIDDLE *Allocasuarina littoralis* rises above the house on an embankment densely planted with *Lomandra longifolia* 'Tanika' and *Phormium tenax* 'Anna Red', which love the extra moisture.

RIGHT Laundry doors can be beautiful too. Stone step with *Lomandra longifolia* 'Tanika' and *Melaleuca nesophila*. The seed pods of *Koelreuteria paniculata* above it rattle in the wind, like falling rain on a roof.

ABOVE The brief was for the house to be hidden amongst trees and garden. Soft layers of planting are delivered by established eucalypts and pines behind, to a middle storey of *Callistemon viminalis* 'Hannah Ray', *Eucalyptus macrandra*, *Allocasuarina littoralis* and *Koelreuteria paniculata* to drifts of tussocks and ground covers.

TERRACED RIVER VIEW

TOORAK

OWNERS
Missy and Nick

LOCATION
Inner suburban Melbourne

SITE DESCRIPTION
Steeply sloping, open

ARCHITECT & DATE
Rob Kennon Architects, new house, 2013

PROPERTY SIZE
870 m²

GARDEN DESIGNED & IMPLEMENTED
2011/2013

The garden spaces of this steep site are generous and the planting bold, to balance the tall, modern off-form concrete house, which steps up the site over four levels. The house and the views from it are framed by *Lagerstroemia indica* x *fauriei* 'Natchez', *Jacaranda mimosifolia* and *Ginkgo biloba* trees; the latter two are repeated in the rear garden for continuity.

A kitchen garden next to the entrance to the property contains an assortment of citrus and *Malus domestica* 'Pink Lady' trees. Rosemary, English lavender and culinary herbs and vegetables grow in large, raised planter boxes surrounded by paths of fine granite gravel into which vegetables and herbs self-seed. This area of the garden receives maximum sunlight and connects strongly with foot traffic in the street, encouraging plenty of conversation with passers-by. It is a source of much pleasure and produce, and beneficial insects abound.

The entrance path to the front door is through a chunky timber gate to a flight of floating concrete platforms with single timber steps in between. This pathway is softened by *Lagerstroemia indica* x *fauriei* 'Natchez' plus bold textural plants such as *Phormium tenax* and *Lomandra longifolia* 'Tanika', and shaped balls of the grey foliaged *Teucrium fruticans*. At night this planting is uplit to create a safe yet intriguing path to the front door. Flanking the house and growing along the northern and southern boundaries is *Bambusa textilis* var. *Gracilis*. Essentially in planter boxes, due to the substantial excavation that occurred on site, this fast-growing clumping bamboo created a tall evergreen screen to neighbouring buildings. It sways in the breeze and produces the most delightful rustling sound.

The next level of garden flows directly from the kitchen/living/dining hub. It is a space for eating, outdoor living and play. Large slabs of slate add a strong organic element to help anchor the house to the site. Interplanted *Pratia pedunculata* is tough wearing and green underfoot. *Jacaranda mimosifolia* trees provide welcome dappled shade in summer as well as a spectacular display of blooms in late spring. They have grown quickly into beautiful sculptural shapes that will be pruned to open up their canopies and allow sunlight to reach the plantings underneath.

The elevated pool is softened with the stunning willowy grass *Miscanthus transmorrisonensis*, *Hedychium gardnerianum*, *Anemone hupehensis*, *Iris germanica* and *Daphne odora*. I especially love this semi-evergreen miscanthus for its feathered and enduring flower heads that dance in the wind and create lovely reflections in the water. Their buff colour is the same as that of the concrete house walls and connects the two.

Above this is the pool garden, dotted with a mini forest of Himalayan birches *Betula utilis* var. *jacquemontii* planted both in the lawn and garden beds. *Nandina domestica*, evergreen *Magnolia* x *grandiflora* 'Little Gem' and *Camellia sasanqua* 'Setsugekka' blur the boundaries and obscure undesirable views. Underplantings of hellebore, ajuga, iris, anemone, hydrangea and more miscanthus provide a continuum of foliage texture and flower colour at different times of the year.

LEFT The top storey is softened with a generous planter box of *Crassula arborescens* 'Bluebird' and gives views from the master bedroom a green frame. Trees help anchor the house to site: *Jacaranda mimosifolia* and *Lagerstroemia indica* x *fauriei* 'Natchez'.

PLANT LIST

TREES

Acer palmatum 'Senkaki'	coral bark maple
Betula utilis var. *jacquemontii*	Himalayan birch
Brugmansia suaveolens	angel's trumpet
Citrus x *limon* 'Eureka'	lemon
Citrus x *sinensis* 'Washington Navel'	orange
Ficus edulis	fig
Ginkgo biloba	maidenhair tree
Jacaranda mimosifolia	jacaranda
Lagerstroemia indica x *fauriei* 'Natchez'	crepe myrtle
Laurus nobilis	bay
Malus domestica 'Pink Lady'	apple
Malus 'Golden Hornet'	crabapple

SHRUBS, SUBSHRUBS

Camellia sasanqua 'Setsugekka'	sasanqua camellia
Ceratostigma willmottianum 'Alba'	Tibetan plumbago
Cotoneaster dammeri	bearberry cotoneaster
Daphne odora	winter daphne
Hydrangea quercifolia	oak-leaf hydrangea
Lavandula angustifolia	English lavender
Magnolia x *grandiflora* 'Little Gem'	evergreen magnolia
Murraya paniculata	orange jessamine
Nandina domestica	sacred bamboo
Rhaphiolepis indica 'Oriental Pearl'	
Rosmarinus officinalis	rosemary

BAMBOO

Bambusa textilis var. *gracilis*	slender weavers bamboo

PERENNIALS, SUCCULENTS, GROUND COVERS

Ajuga reptans 'Jungle Beauty'	bugleweed
Anemone hupehensis	Japanese windflower
Crassula arborescens 'Blue Bird'	
Hedera canariensis	Canary Island ivy
Hedychium gardnerianum	Kahili ginger lily
Helleborus niger 'Josef Lemper'	winter rose
Plectranthus caninus	dogsbane
Pratia pedunculata	trailing pratia
Scaevola aemula 'Pink Ribbon'	fan flower

TUSSOCKS, STRAPPIES

Beschorneria yuccoides	Mexican lily
Dietes bicolor	yellow wild iris
Iris germanica	bearded iris
Lomandra longifolia	spiny-head mat-rush
Miscanthus transmorrisonensis	evergreen miscanthus
Phormium tenax	New Zealand flax

CLIMBERS

Parthenocissus henryana	silver vein creeper

ABOVE Balled *Raphiolepis indica* 'Oriental Pearl', *Phormium tenax*, a leafless *Ginkgo biloba*, *Lagerstroemia indica* x *fauriei* 'Natchez', with *Bambusa textilis* var. *gracilis* behind, *Nandina domestica* and *Brugmansia suaveolens* in the foreground lead to the front door.

244

ABOVE *Bambusa textilis* var. *gracilis* screens the pool garden. Billowing *Miscanthus transmorrisonensis* is repeated among *Betula utilis* var. *jacquemontii* and *Ginkgo biloba* – a strong, simple planting in front of the pool house.

TERRACED RIVER VIEW

THE GARDENS

LEFT A vegetable garden was created in the sunny and open front garden, screened from the street by a hedge of *Murraya paniculata*. *Jacaranda mimosifolia* lessens the overlooking from neighbouring apartments.

ABOVE A feature tree of *Lagerstroemia indica* x *fauriei* 'Natchez', with its cinnamon trunk, is underplanted by *Phormium tenax*, balls of *Teucrium fruticans* and *Raphiolepis indica* 'Oriental Pearl'.

ABOVE Slate steppers with *Pratia pedunculata* in between, as a soft pavement beneath *Jacaranda mimosifolia,* with *Plectranthus caninus* in foreground. The view over the swimming pool to the pool house is lit up by autumn trees.

RIGHT *Bambusa textilis* var. *gracilis,* a self-seeded fig tree (pruned up) and *Miscanthus transmorrisonensis* cascade over the pool creating a green oasis.

TERRACED RIVER VIEW

WALLED DUNE TOP

ST ANDREWS BEACH

OWNERS

Wendy and Peter

LOCATION

St Andrews Beach, Mornington Peninsula

SITE DESCRIPTION

Large, oceanside, open, sandy

ARCHITECT & DATE

Whiting Architects, extension and renovation, 2017

PROPERTY SIZE

8020 m²

GARDEN DESIGNED & IMPLEMENTED

2017/2018

This linear site high on a windswept piece of bushland overlooking Bass Strait was not dissimilar in its topography, size and relationship to the ocean as our own property Karkalla in nearby Sorrento. These commonalities provided a wealth of experience to draw upon.

Mainly covered in *Leptospermum laevigatum* scrub, the soils were sandy and hydrophobic and there was little protection from the prevailing onshore south-westerly winds. In the lee of the dune, on the north side, the owners requested a welcoming entrance and the replanting of many areas with local indigenous species as well as a large vegetable garden for food and flowers. The challenges in achieving this included rabbit predation along with the poor soils and strong winds. The solution lay in creating a walled kitchen garden. Tall off-form concrete walls were designed that extended the architecture into the landscape to provide shelter and maximise solar radiation for this modern take on an English walled garden.

The walls were also an opportunity to espalier many species of citrus, pomegranate and pome fruit trees. Recycled pickets were used to close the openings between the walls and provide a softer link with the timbered landscape beyond. For vegetable, herb and flower growing, long elevated pine planter boxes were built for ease of gardening and to contain the enriched soils needed for growing these hungry plants. Compost bins were also incorporated to recycle the garden and kitchen waste. Slate from central Victoria was used to crazy pave the nearby bedroom terrace and as stepping stones amongst the planters.

Adjacent to the house and to the east of the walled garden lies the remodelled swimming pool. Benched into the landscape by a simple timber retaining wall, the pool is sheltered but with views to the north. Weathered timber decking surrounds the pool and reinforces the nature of its oceanside location. The planting here is a combination of local indigenous plants along with olives and succulent species such as *Cotyledon orbiculata*, with its silvery paddle-shaped leaves, *Kumara plicatilis* (syn. *Aloe*) and the single-stemmed *Aeonium arborescens* which provide leaf contrast and fodder for birds and insects. Honeyeaters love to collect nectar from the bells of the winter flowering cotyledons and aloes. Identifying the entrance to the house are single feature trees of *Banksia integrifolia*, happily growing in the local granitic gravel and providing beautiful organic contrasts with the striped patterning of the off-form concrete walls.

The windward side of the house offers fine ocean views, and these are carefully framed by gnarled *Leptospermum laevigatum* and offset by dynamic seas of shrubs and tussocks, both naturally occurring and planted. A straight sandy path leads down to the beach through the dunes.

This is a garden where the design has been strictly guided by the naturally occurring site conditions: nature is both actively included and selectively excluded.

LEFT Carefully positioned off-form concrete walls extend the house into the landscape and provide a walled enclosure for the kitchen garden. *Cotyledon orbiculata* in foreground, with *Aeonium arborescens, Alyxia buxifolia, Dianella revoluta* var. *brevicaulis* and olive trees. All enjoy similar conditions and thrive without much intervention

PLANT LIST

TREES

Banksia integrifolia	coast banksia
Ficus edulis	fig
Olea europaea	olive
Malus domestica (espalier)	apple
Prunus armeniaca 'Moorpark'	apricot
Prunus persica	peach
Prunus persica var. *nucipersica*	nectarine
Prunus salicina	blood plum
Punica granatum (espalier)	pomegranate

SHRUBS, SUBSHRUBS

Aloysia citrodora	lemon verbena
Alyxia buxifolia	sea box
Correa alba	white correa
Correa 'Marian's Marvel'	native fuchsia
Cotoneaster dammeri	bearberry cotoneaster
Lavandula angustifolia	English lavender
Lavandula dentata	French lavender
Leucophyta brownii	cushion bush
Olearia lanuginosa	woolly daisy bush
Pomaderris paniculosa subsp. *paralia*	coast pomaderris
Rosmarinus officinalis 'Blue Lagoon'	rosemary
Rosmarinus officinalis var. *prostratus*	prostrate rosemary
Salvia mexicana 'Limelight'	Mexican sage
Salvia officinalis	common sage

PERENNIALS, SUCCULENTS, GROUND COVERS

Aeonium arborescens	tree aeonium
Aeonium undulatum	stalked aeonium
Carpobrotus rossii	pigface
Cotyledon orbiculata	pig's ear
Kumara plicatilis	fan aloe
Phlomis fruticosa	Jerusalem sage

TUSSOCKS, STRAPPIES

Austrostipa stipoides	prickly spear-grass
Dianella revoluta var. *brevicaulis*	coast flax lily
Iris germanica	bearded iris
Lepidosperma gladiatum	coast sword-sedge
Lomandra longifolia	spiny-head mat-rush
Poa poiformis var. *ramifer*	dune poa

CLIMBERS

Passiflora edulis	passionfruit

LEFT Recycled timber screens link concrete walls and allow views beyond. An espaliered pomegranate faces north-west and the raised planter beds in the kitchen garden.

MIDDLE *Cotyledon orbiculata, Alyxia buxifolia, Aeonium* and *Dianella revoluta* var. *brevicaulis* fill the curved beds which edge the visitor car parking area.

RIGHT View from the pool area, westwards to the kitchen garden. Local plants *Correa alba, Olearia lanuginosa, Rhagodia condolleana, Leucopogon parviflorus* and old tea-tree form a matrix of colour, form and texture.

255

ABOVE Looking north over the kitchen garden. Slate stepping stones in gravel
lead the eye outwards and provide a dry path in winter walk to the visitor car park
behind the timber screen. Orchard trees are to the left and picking flowers, mainly
roses, to the right.

WALLED DUNE TOP

LEFT & ABOVE Northwest-facing walls are taken up with climbing passionfruit, an espaliered pomegranate and roses. Vegetables are grown in raised beds for ease of harvest.

RIGHT A haven for insects and humans, with mixed herbs, fruit trees and vegetables. There is always something to eat, pick or admire.

WALLED DUNE TOP

ABOVE & RIGHT *Banksia integrifolia* marks the break in the walls for the kitchen garden gate, with slate steppers to and through the approach. The *Banksia integrifolia* throws beautiful shadows and will add sculptural form with time.

WALLED DUNE TOP

CITY
COURTYARD

SOUTH YARRA

OWNERS

Alison and James

LOCATION

Inner suburban Melbourne

SITE DESCRIPTION

Small, shaded, divided

ARCHITECT & DATE

O'Connor Houle Architecture + Landscape, renovation and extension, 2016

PROPERTY SIZE

480 m²

GARDEN DESIGNED & IMPLEMENTED

2016

The gardens at this property were created around an existing two-storey Victorian terrace house, renovated in 2016. The rear garden faces north and contains a double garage that abuts the laneway; this structure and orientation gave us the opportunity to create a roof garden. This elevated garden is best seen from the upstairs master suite and helps frame the view toward the CBD of Melbourne.

The challenges of this site were mainly due to the shade cast by the adjacent house to the west and its mature *Pyrus ussuriensis* trees. Deep shade in some areas has made it difficult to achieve successful or consistent planting.

The rear courtyard is the sunniest space for outside living and an off-form concrete fireplace and chimney, designed by the architect, is the main built feature in this area. It was important from the outset to 'green' the boundaries of this space to make it feel like a lush retreat from the city nearby but not confined by its four walls.

Interest is created within the courtyard by textured, sawn bluestone paving arranged in stripes, with *Pratia pedunculata* in between. This creates a functional, patterned green surface that looks and feels gentler than full hard paving. Walls are utilised as vertical green spaces with self-clinging *Pathenocissus henryana* and *P. tricuspidata* for their autumn leaf colour and summer lushness and espaliered *Camellia sasanqua* 'Hiryu'. The main tree species is *Lagerstroemia indica* x *faurei* 'Natchez', chosen for its small to medium size and the interest it provides through the year – spectacular white frilly flowers in summer, rich bronze-red autumn foliage and smooth cinnamon coloured bark. Once established it is drought tolerant. As the three feature specimens in this garden have matured we have crown thinned them to allow more light through and directed branch growth for form.

Centre stage in the rear garden is a *Hymenosporum flavum*, which will provide heavenly perfumed soft yellow flowers with time. The underplanting was selected predominantly for its foliage attributes, both textural and colour, and shade tolerance. Dainty but tough *Raphiolepis* 'Oriental Pearl', *Arthropodium cirratum* 'Matapouri Bay' and hellebores all perform well; where it is sunny, *Canna* x *generalis* 'Tropicanna', a thriving *Plumeria rubra*, *Citrus* x *latifolia* and culinary herbs grow happily.

In contrast, the roof garden site is a much warmer and windier spot, where soil depth is minimised by necessity. The planting here is all about airy movement. Voluminous tussocks like *Miscanthus transmorrisonensis* and a *Cotoneaster salicifolius*, that throws out willowy arms, dance in the breeze and connect the roof garden to the broader scene. Low-growing *Cotoneaster dammeri* is planted along the threshold of the roof and trails down, connecting the two areas visually.

The interior and exterior areas are strongly married through large openings and by using colours and textures common to both. This is a garden for a grown family, two French bulldogs and friends. It makes its own pictures and doesn't rely heavily on maintenance and care to keep it looking interesting and healthy.

LEFT *Parthenocissus henryana* softens the large east boundary wall with citrus trees and herbs beneath. Facing the door is *Plumeria rubra* var. *acutifolia*.

PLANT LIST

TREES

Citrus x latifolia	Tahitian lime
Hymenosporum flavum	native frangipani
Lagerstroemia indica x fauriei 'Natchez'	crepe myrtle
Plumeria rubra var. *acutifolia*	frangipani

SHRUBS, SUBSHRUBS

Camellia sasanqua 'Hiryu'	sasanqua camellia
Cotoneaster dammeri	bearberry cotoneaster
Cotoneaster salicifolius	willow leaf cotoneaster
Daphne odora	winter daphne
Fatsia japonica	Japanese aralia
Gardenia florida	fragrant gardenia
Hydrangea quercifolia	oak-leaf hydrangea
Mahonia japonica	Japanese mahonia
Monstera deliciosa	Swiss cheese plant
Rhaphiolepis indica 'Spring Pearl'	Indian hawthorn
Rosmarinus officinalis	rosemary

PERENNIALS, SUCCULENTS, GROUND COVERS

Ajuga reptans	bugleweed
Alocasia macrorrhiza	elephant ears
Canna x generalis 'Tropicanna'	canna lily
Dichondra argentea 'Silver Falls'	silver nickel vine
Hedychium gardnerianum	Kahili ginger lily
Pratia pedunculata	trailing pratia

TUSSOCKS, STRAPPIES

Arthropodium cirratum 'Matapouri Bay'	New Zealand rock lily
Cordyline stricta	slender palm lily
Lomandra longifolia 'Tanika'	spiny-head mat-rush
Miscanthus transmorrisonensis	evergreen miscanthus

CLIMBERS

Parthenocissus henryana	silver vein creeper
Parthenocissus tricuspidata	Boston Ivy
Solandra maxima	golden chalice vine
Trachelospermum jasminoides	star jasmine

ABOVE The garage roof garden with views towards the city is planted with tussocks of *Lomandra longifolia* 'Tanika', *Cotoneaster salicifolia*, *Raphiolepis indica* 'Spring Pearl' and *Miscanthus transmorrisonensis* to provide height to soften neighbouring buildings. All these plants thrive with little soil depth. A bird bath was added for wildlife and the area mulched with Ovens River pebbles.

ABOVE *Plumeria rubra* var. *acutifolia* provides summer perfume in the courtyard
while neighbouring deciduous trees give summer shade and allow winter light.
Camellia sasanqua is espaliered on walls and *Parthenocissus henryana* rambles
between, to blur the boundaries of this small space.

RIGHT *Pratia pedunculata* grows between sawn bluestone pavers. Even this tiny addition adds texture and greenery to the courtyard, and the feeling is garden space, not paved space.

LEFT Entry to the courtyard garden from the rear of the property. The roof garden is visible above the garage.

MIDDLE The rooftop garden is an oasis in this inner urban setting and absorbs rainfall and reduces temperatures.

RIGHT Over time, *Hymenosporum flavum* will balance the height of the garage wall behind sculptural *Lagerstroemia indica x fauriei*, its bare branches echoing the colour of the autumnal *Parthenocissus henryana* and neighbouring red brick wall. *Canna* x *generalis* 'Tropicanna' grows alongside the path. This is definitely a seasonal garden, with plants that thrive in a range of conditions.

THE GARDENS

ABOVE A view through to the rear courtyard. *Solandra maxima* grows on the garage corner, its large chalice-shaped yellow blooms providing heavenly perfume in the summer evenings. The faded seed heads of *Lagerstroemia indica x fauriei* add texture right through winter.

RIGHT The north-west facing rooftop garden with the master bedroom beyond.

SHADED HIDEAWAY

TOORAK

OWNERS

Helen and Campbell

LOCATION

Inner suburban Melbourne

SITE DESCRIPTION

Large, sloping, clayey

ARCHITECT & DATE

de Campo Architects, new house, 2005

PROPERTY SIZE

1720 m²

GARDEN DESIGNED & IMPLEMENTED

2006

The requirements for this family's outdoor space were somewhere for the children to play and 'get lost', to integrate the swimming pool and an in-ground trampoline, some screening of the neighbours' houses, an area for herbs and vegetables and inclusion of some plants from the owners' New Zealand homeland.

To create some level, useable areas a high retaining wall on the front boundary was necessary. It was important to soften this physical barrier to the street with soft plantings both on and above the wall. This was achieved with *Callistemon pallidus* 'White Cloud' and clambering *Parthenocissus tricuspidata* 'Lowii'.

The garden is a series of spaces with different purposes linked, in the most part, by a lawn. Much of the planting in this front area is boldly designed: large clumps of *Phormium tenax* 'Anna Red', mass planting of single species such as *Pennisetum alopecuroides* and *Arthropodium cirratum*, large walls of the evergreen *Myrtus communis*, copses of *Eucalyptus pauciflora* 'Little Snowman' and fast-growing *Cotinus coggygria* 'Grace'. The robust scale of this planting balances the house and creates a wildness that suggests that not all is under control. The trampoline is hidden here and the pool projects out into this lower garden space too, its concrete edge anchored by drifts of plants and the overhead canopies of nearby trees, which hold the pool in the landscape rather than shading it. This is a strong marriage of architecture and garden.

Adjacent to the house a shady spot for outdoor dining and relaxing has been created. This area is shaded by a *Jacaranda mimosifolia* and enclosed with a hedge of *Murraya paniculata* with *Cordyline species* projecting out of its dark green surface to create drama.

Behind the house and to the south-east lies a pergola-covered courtyard, simply gravelled in the style of the French. It is adjacent to the kitchen, so large, galvanised steel and spotted gum planter boxes were made to grow herbs and vegetables.

Copses of *Betula utilis* var. *jacquemontii* underplanted with *Bartlettina sordida* have worked well next to the driveway, with its yellow clay and an excess of underground and surface water. The pure white trunks contrast beautifully with the large dark leaves of the *Bartlettina sordida*, its fluffy blooms heralding spring. This is a favourite part of the garden for the owners, seen from their home office.

Fourteen years since its creation, this garden has developed its own patina. As trees have grown and shade increased, some of the underplanting has needed updating to more shade tolerant species, such as replacing *Anigozanthos* 'Big Red', once a spectacular feature of the front garden, with *Arthropodium cirratum*. Trees are continually crown thinned and shaped to become sculptural elements. This is a garden that is very much about the beauty of trees: the shadows they create, seasonal changes and textured trunks.

LEFT A pedestrian path to the front door is made of simple concrete pavers and provides pattern and rhythm. Billowing *Pennisetum alopecuroides* edges the path, contrasting with the dark green of the clipped *Myrtus communis*. Texture to the right of the path comes from a hedged *Acca sellowiana*.

PLANT LIST

TREES

Acca sellowiana	feijoa
Angophora costata	smooth-barked apple
Betula utilis var. jacquemontii	Himalayan birch
Brachychiton populneus	kurrajong
Citrus x latifolia	Tahitian lime
Citrus x limon 'Eureka'	lemon
Elaeocarpus reticulatus	blueberry ash
Eucalyptus pauciflora 'Little Snowman'	snow gum
Jacaranda mimosifolia	jacaranda
Murraya paniculata	orange jessamine

SHRUBS, SUBSHRUBS

Bartlettina sordida	blue mist flower
Callistemon pallidus 'White Cloud'	lemon bottlebrush
Cordyline species	cabbage tree
Correa reflexa var. nummulariifolia	roundleaf correa
Cotinus coggygria 'Grace'	smokebush
Cotoneaster dammeri	bearberry cotoneaster
Daphne odora	winter daphne
Melianthus major	cape honey flower
Myrtus communis	common myrtle
Nandina domestica	sacred bamboo

PERENNIALS, SUCCULENTS, GROUND COVERS

Alocasia macrorrhiza	elephant ears
Asparagus densiflorus 'Myersii'	foxtail fern
Hedychium coronarium	white ginger lily
Hedychium gardnerianum	Kahili ginger lily

BAMBOO

Bambusa oldhamii	oldham bamboo

TUSSOCKS, STRAPPIES

Arthropodium cirratum 'Matapouri Bay'	New Zealand rock lily
Dietes bicolor	yellow wild iris
Liriope 'Evergreen Giant'	giant lily-turf
Pennisetum alopecuroides	Chinese fountain grass
Phormium tenax	New Zealand flax
Phormium tenax 'Anna Red'	New Zealand flax

CLIMBERS

Parthenocissus tricuspidata 'Lowii'	Boston ivy
Vitis vinifera	grape vine

ABOVE Bare trunks of *Betula utilis* var. *jacquemontii* allow light into the owners' study in winter and is a strong contrast with the leaves of *Bartlettina sordida*, whose giant mauve flowers in spring provide interest before new leaves appear on the birches. *Liriope* 'Evergreen Giant' provide texture at the base. A simple, strong planting of three species only.

ABOVE *Jacaranda mimosifolia* delivers summer shade and early summer blooms in front of the strong green hedges of *Murraya paniculata*. *Cordyline species* break the surface of the hedge for textural contrast. A huge slab of salvaged river red gum has been used in a table designed by Ben Wrigley.

LEFT *Cordyline species, Murraya paniculata* hedge and the feathery foliage of *Jacaranda mimosifolia* overhead.

MIDDLE The sculptured trunks of *Eucalyptus pauciflora* 'Little Snowman' frame the pool, their organic forms deliberately used to interrupt the strong lines of architecture. *Pennisetum alopecuroides* adds soft.

RIGHT Recycled timber batten fencing is a textured backdrop to *Dietes bicolor* and the large leaves of *Alocasia macrorrhiza,* both thriving in shade of huge neighbouring *Ulmus parvifolia.* A copper birdbath made from a recycled hot-water unit adds whimsy and water.

LEFT *Bambusa oldhamii* was added next to the cubby in a hidden corner of the garden for additional privacy.

RIGHT Concrete pavers sweep around to the pool terrace. *Eucalyptus pauciflora* 'Little Snowman', with their bendy trunks and mottled bark, dot the lawn, next to the well-shaped *Myrtus communis* hedge. *Plectranthus ecklonii* flowers in the shade, with *Arthropodium cirratum* providing waist-height clumps of green.

ABOVE *Brachychiton populneus* as a feature tree for form and flowers, *Asparagus meyersii* for their vivid green tails, plus *Cotinus coggygria* 'Grace' (at right) for flowers and foliage. *Phormium tenax* 'Anna Red' edges out of the canopy, next to *Pennisetum alopecuroides*. These are big expressions of plants to match the scale of the house and garden.

SHADED HIDEAWAY

BELOW *Eucalyptus pauciflora* 'Little Snowman' trunks match the colour of house but contrasts strongly in shape and line.

RIGHT Copses of *Betula utilis* var. *jacquemontii,* at the end of their autumn glory, underpinned with solid green plantings of *Bartlettina sordida* and *Liriope* 'Evergreen Giant'.

THE GARDENS

NATIVE RIDGE TOP

FLINDERS

OWNERS

Julie and Paul

LOCATION

Flinders Ridge, Mornington Peninsula

SITE DESCRIPTION

Sloping site near ocean

ARCHITECT & DATE

Inarc Architects, new house, 2011/2012

PROPERTY SIZE

1860 m²

GARDEN DESIGNED & IMPLEMENTED

2011

Overlooking the entrance to Western Port and Phillip Island to the south-east and pasturelands to the north-west, this beach house sits high on the site, on a bluff. This created a very steep embankment on the coast-facing side to revegetate and a warm sun trap at the front for outdoor sitting and dining areas, a vegetable garden and swimming pool. The owners had a wish list of Australian plants to use, both indigenous to the area and from further afield.

The site's clayey soil and areas of groundwater required careful consideration in the design approach. The slope at the rear was quickly stabilised with indigenous plants, which took hold readily in their weed mat. Three large existing eucalypts frame views of the ocean, provide a refuge for birdlife and perfectly balance the height of the two-storey home.

Planting on the sunny side is designed to complement and balance the pale blue void of the pool, tucked into the site for protection, with a level area adjacent for pool lounging. At differing times of the day the water reflects the surrounding plant textures and colours, creating another layer of views. Pride of place is held by

a towering *Eucalyptus leucoxylon* 'Rosea', its canopy connecting the house to the landscape and its grey mottled trunk reflecting the colours of the house. A small kitchen garden for herbs and vegetables has been established in large round concrete planters, along with a few fruit trees within easy access from the house.

The planting design on this side of the property falls into two groupings. Where the heavier soils and groundwater remain, *Doryanthes excelsa*, *Allocasuarina littoralis*, *Callistemon* 'Kings Park Special', *C. viminalis* 'Little John' and *Grevillea rhyolitica* 'Deua Flame' all thrive. Where the area is terraced, and the soil better drained, species such as *Banksia spinulosa*, *B. integrifolia*, *Leucadendron* 'Safari Sunset', *Anigozanthos* 'Big Red' and pine-leaved geebung *Persoonia pinifolia* act as feature plants. The kitchen, living and dining areas are positioned to enjoy views of these spaces, so it was important to consider design from a bird's eye view and from within the garden areas themselves. The plant palette provides foliage interest, bird and insect habitat and a richly diverse setting for a couple who enjoy observing nature and seasonal change.

LEFT Existing large eucalypts in the embankment to the south anchor the garden and balance the scale of the building. The bank is stabilised with a variety of bird- and insect-attracting shrubs and tussocks and which blur the boundary between the garden proper and landscape beyond.

PLANT LIST

TREES

Agonis flexuosa 'Burgundy'	burgundy willow myrtle
Allocasuarina littoralis	black she-oak
Banksia integrifolia	coast banksia
Citrus x latifolia	Tahitian lime
Eucalyptus forrestiana	fuchsia gum
Ficus edulis	fig
Leptospermum brachyandrum 'Silver'	silver weeping tea-tree
Prunus armeniaca 'Moorpark'	apricot

SHRUBS, SUBSHRUBS

Banksia ericifolia	heath-leaved banksia
Bauera rubioides var. *alba*	white river rose
Callistemon 'Kings Park Special'	bottlebrush
Callistemon viminalis 'Little John'	bottlebrush
Correa alba	white correa
Correa pulchella var. *minor*	native fuchsia
Correa reflexa 'Kangaroo Island'	Kangaroo Island fuchsia
Correa reflexa var. *nummulariifolia*	roundleaf correa
Grevillea 'Moonlight'	
Grevillea longistyla	long-styled grevillea
Grevillea rhyolitica 'Deua Flame'	
Hakea salicifolia	willow-leaved hakea
Lavandula angustifolia	English lavender
Leptospermum flavescens 'Cardwell'	tea-tree
Leucadendron 'Safari Sunset'	
Persoonia pinifolia	geebung
Protea 'Pink Ice'	
Rhagodia candolleana	seaberry saltbush
Thryptomene saxicola	rock thryptomene

PERENNIALS, SUCCULENTS, GROUND COVERS

Dichondra argentea 'Silver Falls'	silver nickel vine
Goodenia elongata	lanky goodenia
Scaevola albida 'White Carpet'	fan flower

RIGHT The pool is surrounded by a sea of tussocks and ground covers, with the existing large *Eucalyptus* providing a focal point. *Lomandra longifolia* 'Tanika', *Correa reflexa* var. *nummulariifolia* and *Scaevola albida* 'White Carpet' are used with larger shrubs behind to disguise the eastern boundary fence.

TUSSOCKS, STRAPPIES

Anigozanthos 'Big Red'; 'Cross of Gold'; 'Orange Cross'	kangaroo paw
Dianella revoluta var. *brevicaulis*	coast flax lily
Dianella tasmanica	Tasman flax lily
Doryanthes excelsa	gymea lily
Lomandra longifolia 'Tanika'	spiny-head mat-rush
Poa poiformis var. *ramifer*	dune poa
Themeda triandra 'True Blue'	kangaroo grass

CLIMBERS

Pandorea jasminoides 'Lady Di'	bower of beauty vine

NATIVE RIDGE TOP

ABOVE The brief requested a variety of native Australian plants that my clients had previously grown and enjoyed and as many as possible were designed into their new garden. *Correa reflexa* var. *nummulariifolia* and *Lomandra longifolia* 'Tanika' fill the foreground, and *Thryptomene saxicola* encircles the base of the *Eucalyptus*. Banksias and bottlebrushs appear behind, as well as spikes of *Doryanthes excelsa*. *Protea* 'Pink Ice' and *Allocasuarina littoralis* are layered in the centre.

NATIVE RIDGE TOP

LEFT The house is anchored to the garden setting by the large eucalypts on site.
Tussocks and ground covers provide a soft surround to the pool.

MIDDLE The gravel surface of the steep driveway is held in place with large, recycled beams of timber. *Allocasuarina littoralis* and *Banksia integrifolia* frame the approach while tussocks and shrubs spill over the edge of the driveway.

RIGHT Recycled timber and a copper-pipe pool fence gently surround the pool and its soft mantle of planting. Reflections from the planting make beautiful shapes on the water.

THE GARDENS

LEFT Gravel balances a mass of mixed planting. Soft evergreen shapes merge into each other, with the vertical spears of *Doryanthes excelsa* pulling the eye skywards.

ABOVE The embankment in front of the house, which leads down to the pool, is blanketed in *Lomandra longifolia* 'Tanika' and *Callistemon viminalis* 'Little John'. *Leucadendron* 'Safari Sunset' under the eaves is enjoyed as a cut flower.

PARKSIDE JUNGLE

TOORAK

OWNERS

Fiona and David

LOCATION

Inner suburban Melbourne

SITE DESCRIPTION

Small, shady, flat, divided

ARCHITECT & DATE

de Campo Architects, new house, 2011

PROPERTY SIZE

540 m2

GARDEN DESIGNED & IMPLEMENTED

2012

It has been challenging to establish a garden on this site – our Melbourne home – over the last nine years. A park to the east and a reserve abutting the northern boundary offer broad green borrowed landscapes and were the main reason we chose the property; however, they do contain very large trees with voracious root systems, and this has driven careful plant selection.

Our brief to ourselves was somewhere to sit, somewhere for two Jack Russell terriers, somewhere to get wet, some citrus trees, a small number of herbs and vegetables, compost, year-round beauty, seasonal surprises and a blurring of the boundaries.

As you step into the arrival courtyard you are enveloped in green serenity. A large metal water bowl with goldfish and water lilies provides a central focus and reflects the towering *Eucalyptus cladocalyx* trunks behind it. *Tetrapanax papyrifer* creates the overhead canopy, and *Bambusa multiplex* 'Goldstripe' is included for the vibrant patterning of its stems and screening properties. *Camellia sasanqua* 'Hiryu' adds hot-pink bursts in autumn, *Euphorbia lambii* offers architectural form, and *Daphne odora* 'Aureomarginata' for scent. Exposed aggregate concrete has been sandblasted to incorporate all the different colours of this zone, and solid cypress pine front steps used for their silver weathered look.

The side gardens are designed to be viewed from within the home and merge with the main interior living spaces. Windows and doors are the full height of the rooms to enhance this connection and the carpet colours in two instances, as well as the kitchen cabinetry, are shades of green, reflecting the dominant outside colour. *Acer palmatum* 'Senkaki', *Nandina*, *Alocasia macrorrhiza*, white-flowered *Abutilon* x *hybridom*, *Monstera deliciosa*, *Pittosporum tobira* 'Miss Muffet' and dainty *Pratia pedunculata* form the basis of the plant palette. Mike Nicholls' wooden sculpture of a woman hides partially behind foliage.

Interest is created in the slate-paved pool garden at the rear through striking foliage contrasts and flower colour. Citrus trees, a discarded ornamental banana from a client's garden, hot pink *Lagerstroemia indica* x *fauriei* 'Tuscarora' crepe myrtle, orange *canna* x *generalis* 'Tropicanna', yellow *Acacia podalyriifolia* all offer colour at different times of the year and work well alongside the poolside foliage. The concrete tank is an affordable, sculptural and highly effective spot to cool off in during summer. It sits high enough to not require a pool fence and is accessed by a boat ladder.

This is a garden for everyday living for a small family, for dogs, for thirsty birdlife, for friends and clients. It's a casual and easy to care for garden, and for us it is our private oasis from the hustle and bustle of city life.

LEFT The giant *Eucalyptus cladocalyx* in the nature reserve next door is a real presence in this front courtyard; plant species were curated for their ability to grow beneath it. *Nandina domestica*, *Fatsia japonica*, *Lomandra longifolia* 'Tanika', *Euphorbia lambii* and *Alocasia macrorrhiza* all enjoy this site, creating assemblages of leaf texture, colour and size. *Pistacia chinensis* is a wonderful feature tree with its sculptural form and autumn colour.

PLANT LIST

TREES

Acacia podalyriifolia	Mount Morgan wattle
Acer palmatum 'Senkaki'	coral-bark maple
Brugmansia suaveolens	angel's trumpet
Citrus x latifolia	Tahitian lime
Citrus x limon 'Eureka'	lemon
Citrus x sinensis 'Washington Navel'	orange
Ensete sp.	Abyssinian banana
Lagerstroemia indica x fauriei 'Tuscarora'	crepe myrtle
Pistacia chinensis	Chinese pistachio

SHRUBS, SUBSHRUBS

Abutilon x hybridum	Chinese lantern
Camellia sasanqua 'Hiryu'	sasanqua camellia
Chimonanthus praecox	wintersweet
Cotoneaster dammeri	bearberry cotoneaster
Cotoneaster horizontalis	rock cotoneaster
Daphne odora 'Aureomarginata'	gold-edged winter daphne
Fatsia japonica	Japanese aralia
Hydrangea macrophylla var. *normalis*	white lacecap hydrangea
Hydrangea quercifolia	oak-leaf hydrangea
Nandina domestica	sacred bamboo
Pelargonium tomentosum	peppermint geranium
Pittosporum tobira 'Miss Muffet'	
Tetrapanax papyrifer	rice-paper plant
Viburnum carlesii	Korean spice viburnum

BAMBOO

Bambusa multiplex 'Goldstripe'	goldstripe bamboo

PERENNIALS, SUCCULENTS, GROUND COVERS

Ajuga reptans 'Jungle Beauty'	bugleweed
Alocasia macrorrhiza	elephant ears
Asplenium nidus	bird's nest fern
Canna x generalis 'Tropicanna'	canna lily
Epiphyllum sp.	orchid cactus
Lamium galeobdolon	aluminium plant
Monstera deliciosa	Swiss cheese plant
Plectranthus ambiguus 'Nico'	
Pratia pedunculata	trailing pratia

TUSSOCKS, STRAPPIES

Clivia nobilis	green-tip forest lily
Dianella tasmanica	Tasman flax lily
Lomandra longifolia 'Tanika'	spiny-head mat-rush
Miscanthus transmorrisonensis	evergreen miscanthus

CLIMBERS

Parthenocissus quinquefolia	Virginia creeper
Solandra maxima 'Variegata'	chalice vine

ABOVE Looking down on the front garden from the bathroom terrace.
Next to the deep orange of *Clivia nobilis* is *Hydrangea macrophylla* var.
normalis in bloom, repeated around the garden.

ABOVE The view through the front gate to tall *Tetrapanax papyrifer*, with *Alocasia macrorrhiza* and tussocks beneath. In the foreground, the slatted fence is softened by the self-clinging *Parthenocissus quinquefolia*. *Chimonanthus praecox* arches over the gate, providing canopy, and sweet clove-scented flowers in winter.

RIGHT *Parthenocissus quinquefolia* climbs the walls of the house and is a backdrop for *Clivia nobilis*, fragrant *Daphne odorata* 'Aureomarginata', with its gold-edged leaves, *Alocasia macrorrhiza* and *Lomandra longifolia* 'Tanika'.

ABOVE The view east towards the park. We've screened the lower views of the road with a timber batten fence, sections arranged vertically and horizontally, and carefully placed shrubs of *Camellia sasanqua*, *Brugmansia suaveolens*, *Bambusa multiplex* 'Gold Stripe' and *Tetrapanax papyrifer*.

PARKSIDE JUNGLE

LEFT The rear garden courtyard is paved with crazy slate, which picks up the colours in the house and pool wall. *Lagerstroemia indica* x *fauriei* 'Tuscarora' provides important summer shade and, by lifting its canopy, a view is maintained from inside the house to this rear garden area. *Pittosporum tobira* 'Miss Muffet' sits at its base.

MIDDLE The sky is reflected in the large steel bowl used as a fishpond in the front courtyard. The summer blooms of *Hydrangea macrophylla* var. *normalis* brighten the shaded space and *Tetrapanax papyrifer* reaches high over a home-made bench.

RIGHT The tiled concrete tank pool, with its granite steps, plays a sculptural role in the rear garden and is a shining blue jewel from above. *Acacia podalyriifolia* drops its fluffy yellow flowers onto the pool surface in mid-winter creating a spectacular scene.

LEFT In the front courtyard, stacked beams of cypress pine form the steps to the house. A simple Japanese aesthetic is achieved with large river pebbles blanketing the ground under the *Pistacia chinensis*.

MIDDLE A Mike Nicholls' timber sculpture creates a focal point from the dining room, framed between *Abutilon* x *hybridum*, with its white bells, and *Acer palmatum* 'Senkaki', selected for its lush green leaves and stunning autumn foliage.

RIGHT With a deep green carpet in the living room and floor-to-ceiling windows we are able to bring the garden into the house. *Asplenium nidus, Pittosporum tobira* 'Miss Muffet', *Lamium galeobdolon, Alocasia macrorrhiza* and *Nandina domestica* do well under the reserve's large *Celtis australis* and provide year-round interest in foliage, colour and texture. Views of the reserve are enjoyed from all rooms by choosing lowish growing species.

307

ABOVE The lush green view down the north side of the house. *Dianella tasmanica* backs on to the glass, growing between the slate is two-toned *Lamium galeobdolon* with aromatic *Pelargonium tomentosum* on the opposite side. The large slate steppers lead the eye down to the rear garden courtyard.

ABOVE Large-foliaged plants like *Asplenium nidus* and a large form of *Alcantarea imperialis* 'Silver Plum' in a pot make strong features in a shaded garden setting.

ACKNOWLEDGEMENTS

Creating this book has been some years in the making, as I waited for the time to be right – for our daughters to finish school and for the right mix of examples of our gardens to be ready. And if 'It takes a village to raise a child' the same is true of delivering a book. My grateful thanks go to several special people in this village. First and foremost, to my partner David Swann and his hardworking construction team who bring my gardens to life. Each garden is unique, often in multiple ways, and presents its own set of challenges. Their attention to detail and dedication to a high-quality finish is outstanding and appreciated. I thank the team for their problem-solving and flair.

I would like to acknowledge Brin Jones of Jones Landscapes who built the Bayside Japanese garden with care and expertise. Brin builds many of my gardens and we value his commitment and professionalism.

Many people are involved in the construction of my gardens and their ongoing care and maintenance. Sonja Rosette and Heidi Ross are two such people. The continuous care of many of the gardens featured in this book that they and their teams have provided over the years is highly valued by myself and the garden owners.

To my clients, not only those whose gardens feature in *With Nature*, but to all our clients who have placed their trust in us to create beautiful, functional gardens that meet their needs. It has been a joy. By extension, to the garden carers, whose ongoing role is often undervalued. Gardens stay looking good thanks to the maintenance they receive.

To Ella and Yas, who provided the impetus to create our own haven, Karkalla, with its fairy gardens, bespoke cubby house, rabbit enclosures, billy cart routes and inspiring spaces for exploring.

To photographer Earl Carter, whom I had longed to work with and who has captured the essence of each garden so sensitively through his mastery of light. I couldn't be more thrilled with his beautiful images.

Nicky Pitkanen, who works tirelessly for me, contributed huge slabs of her time to help proofread and 'book wrangle' hundreds of images into their best position in the book. Her commitment to my design practice and her broad range of talents is second to none. Thanks also to Milla Pitkanen, who embarked on the onerous job of typing all that I had written longhand. You will always remember your first job, Milla.

To Laura Dalrymple, one of my oldest and closest friends, whose opinion I value greatly, especially in all things visual and getting to the heart of what is important. Laura preceded me with the publication of her own book *The Ethical Omnivore* and her insights were enormously helpful.

At Hardie Grant, thanks to publisher Pam Brewster and all the team for their enthusiasm and support in bringing this project to fruition. Also to my copy editor Kate Daniel, who undertook the monumental task of making my wanderings with words make sense. Writing is not my strongest suit and Kate was the perfect person to unravel what I had written and refashion it eloquently.

FIONA BROCKHOFF

Fiona Brockhoff is an Australian garden designer whose landscapes are crafted with nature.

Her own garden, created on a windswept sand dune on Victoria's Mornington Peninsula, has been profiled all over the world and is widely regarded as an iconic contemporary garden. Fiona's designs draw on rich plant palettes of foliage colour and form and champion the use of indigenous plants and local materials used sustainably. Her beautiful modern gardens are renown for their strong sense of place, space and texture.

Photograph Kelly Gardener

This edition published in 2022 by Hardie Grant Books,
an imprint of Hardie Grant Publishing
First published in 2022

Hardie Grant Books (Melbourne)
Wurundjeri Country
Building 1, 658 Church Street
Richmond, Victoria 3121

Hardie Grant Books (London)
5th & 6th Floors
52–54 Southwark Street
London SE1 1UN

hardiegrantbooks.com

 A catalogue record for this
book is available from the
National Library of Australia

With Nature
ISBN 9781743796856

10 9 8 7 6 5 4 3 2 1

Publisher: Pam Brewster
Project Editors: Brooke Munday and Joanna Wong
Editor: Kate Daniel
Design Manager: Kristin Thomas
Designer: Evi O. Studio | Evi O and Wilson Leung
Photographer: Earl Carter
Production Manager: Todd Rechner

Colour reproduction by Splitting Image Colour Studio
Printed in China by Leo Paper Products LTD.

The paper this book is printed on is from FSC®-certified forests and other sources.
FSC® promotes environmentally responsible, socially beneficial and economically
viable management of the world's forests.

Hardie Grant acknowledges the Traditional Owners of the country on which we work,
the Wurundjeri people of the Kulin nation and the Gadigal people of the Eora nation,
and recognises their continuing connection to the land, waters and culture. We pay our
respects to their Elders past and present.